9/16/14

SO, YOU WANT To Work in SPORTS?

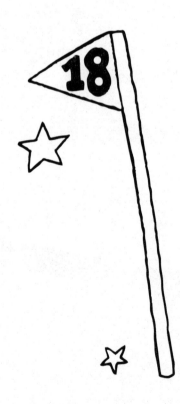

SO, YOU WANT To Work in SPORTS?

The Ultimate Guide to Exploring the SPORTS INDUSTRY

Louisburg Library
Bringing People and Information Together

Joanne Mattern

BE WHAT YOU WANT *Series*

ALADDIN
New York London Toronto Sydney New Delhi

 **BEYOND** WORDS
Hillsboro, Oregon

ALADDIN
An imprint of Simon & Schuster
Children's Publishing Division
1230 Avenue of the Americas
New York, NY 10020

BEYOND WORDS
20827 N.W. Cornell Road, Suite 500
Hillsboro, Oregon 97124-9808
503-531-8700 / 503-531-8773 fax
www.beyondword.com

This Beyond Words/Aladdin edition April 2014
Copyright © 2014 by Beyond Words Publishing
Illustrations copyright © 2014 by iStockphoto.com
Front cover photo copyright © 2014 by Joshua Hodge Photography/E+/Getty Images
Tennis ball, soccer ball, and back jacket photos copyright © 2014 by iStockphoto.com

ALADDIN is a trademark of Simon & Schuster, Inc., and related logo is a registered
trademark of Simon & Schuster, Inc.
Beyond Words is an imprint of Simon & Schuster, Inc. and the Beyond Words logo is
a registered trademark of Beyond Words Publishing, Inc.

For information about special discounts for bulk purchases, please contact
Simon & Schuster Special Sales at 1-866-506-1949 or business@simonandschuster.com.

The Simon & Schuster Speakers Bureau can bring authors to your live event.
For more information or to book an event contact the Simon & Schuster Speakers
Bureau at 1-866-248-3049 or visit our website at www.simonspeakers.com.

Managing Editor: Lindsay S. Brown
Editors: Emmalisa Sparrow, Kristin Thiel
Design: Sara E. Blum
Proofreader: Gretchen Stelter
The text of this book was set in Bembo.

Manufactured in the United States of America 0214 FFG

10 9 8 7 6 5 4 3 2 1

Library of Congress Cataloging-in-Publication Data

Mattern, Joanne.
   So, you want to work in sports? : the ultimate guide to exploring the sports
      industry / Joanne Mattern.
   pages   cm. — (Be what you want)
   Includes bibliographical references.
   1. Sports—Vocational guidance—Juvenile literature. I. Title.
   GV734.3.M37 2014
   796.02'3—dc23
                                                                              2013025469

ISBN 978-1-58270-449-4 (hc)
ISBN 978-1-58270-448-7 (pbk)
ISBN 978-1-4424-9513-5 (eBook)

To uncover your true
potential, you must first
find your own limits, and
then you have to have
the courage to blow
past them.

Picabo Street

SKIER

CONTENTS

1

I Want to Work in Sports! But How?

Close your eyes and imagine some fantastic moments in sports. For a sports fan, there are few things as exciting as hearing the powerful crack of a bat meeting a ball and watching the ball soar over the outfield wall for a home run. Or how about the sheer joy of a seeing a football player muscle his way through a line of defenders, shaking off tackles, the ball cradled in his hands as he runs toward the end zone and a touchdown? Perhaps you get your thrills watching sprinters fly down the track, their legs and arms pumping, or hearing the crash and clatter of skates and sticks as hockey players fight for the puck. Whatever your favorite sport, there are so many amazing emotions, feelings, sights, and sounds. It's no wonder millions of people are rabid sports fans and players.

Many people love sports and are content to sit on the sidelines, cheering on their favorite team, wearing their favorite athlete's jersey, sharing the thrill of victory—and the agony of defeat—with their friends and family. Other people want to go even further. For you, just watching isn't enough. Participating is the key to your sports joy. For you sports lovers, actually participating in the sporting world is the key to your dreams.

If someone asks you to think of a career in sports, what's the first thing that comes to your mind? If you're like most people, you probably think of a professional athlete, like the Major League Baseball (MLB) or National Basketball Association (NBA) players you see on television. For a select few, becoming a superstar athlete on a nationally known professional team is a dream that comes true. However, that isn't the only way to carve out a career in sports. In fact, there are many, many more people who make a living at sports and don't appear on television. You can even have a career in sports without being particularly great at sports yourself!

Sports are played at every level in society. Stop and think about your own community. Your local high schools probably have athletic programs that feature everything from basketball to swimming to cross-country and track. Then there are college sports, local leagues, and sporting clubs. Youth leagues bring young athletes together. So do community organizations like the YMCA and the Boys & Girls Clubs. Whatever your sport, there is probably a local or regional club or team that represents it.

REASONS YOU MAY WANT TO WORK IN SPORTS

A Passion for Playing the Game

Do you love playing a sport? Do you enjoy the challenges of regular practice and improving yourself with each one? Does the roar of the crowd exhilarate you? Are you agile, fast, or strong? The arena, field, or court may be your workplace. Most of you who participate in sports are never going to be big league professionals making millions of dollars and flashing your smiles on television. But that doesn't mean you can't make a living playing sports. For every MLB team, there are multiple levels of minor league farm teams or independent teams. Players on these teams get to play ball every day, hone skills, and get a paycheck. Some of these players move up to the big leagues. Others stay in the minors. Either way, you still get to play ball for a living. Many people would consider that a pretty great lifestyle!

There are also professional sporting options away from home. Many NBA players get their start playing for teams in Europe. The same is true for athletes in other sports, such as soccer. These players get to live in a foreign country, travel a lot, and be part of a team with fans. Some of them make a pretty good living too. Best of all, those of you who do this are working at what you love and getting paid for it.

> In riding a horse, we borrow freedom.
>
> **Helen Thomson**
> SHOW JUMPER

Names: Sisters Jodelle and Abigail Marx
Ages: 14 and 12
Job (when not studying!): Equestrians, Columbia Winds Pony Club, a part of the United States Pony Club, Portland, Oregon
Dream Job: (Jodelle) When I am sixteen, I hope to qualify to represent the United States in an international rally, or competition. By the time I turn twenty-five, I want to be a Graduate "A" Pony Clubber (the highest ranking in

Pony Club). I would like to go into a career with horses, possibly a horse trainer/riding instructor. **(Abigail)** I don't know what my career goals are because I am only twelve, and I have a lot of options to choose from. My goals include, however, becoming an A Pony Clubber, which means that you have completed all the levels of Pony Club—in other words, you are a professional horse person.

What sports have you partici-pated in and when?

Jodelle: I ride horses. Most people think of it as more of a hobby than a sport, so I always ask them, "It is part of the Olympics, isn't it?" There are many different disciplines in horseback riding. I have dabbled in others, but I mainly do eventing, show jumping, and dressage. In elementary school, I played soccer, but I dropped out when I moved to my new school. I've always been an athletic kind of person.

Abigail: I played soccer when I was in kindergarten and a little in first grade, but I have always ridden horses. Even before I could walk, I rode horses. My mom would hold me on when I was about six months old and walk me around the arena on our pony named Rose.

What are you doing now in terms of education/sports participation?

Jodelle: I know that being a good horse owner is knowing as much as possible about horses. That's why when I'm at school, and my teachers say, "Get out your books and read," I don't groan like my classmates. I take the chance to read about something that I know will further my career in the horse world. One time, I was reading a book about the anatomy of the horse, and my social studies teacher leaned over and commented that I always had the weirdest books; I just smiled and kept reading. I also take riding lessons every week and ride my horse at least four other days to keep us on track. During the summer I take my horse to camp to raise both of our experience levels.

Abigail: I am studying for Quiz rally next year. Quiz rally is a competition were Pony Clubbers work together on a team to earn points by answering questions about horses. This year my sister, Jodelle, went to the regional rally [Northwest Region] and qualified to go to championships in Lexington, Virginia; next year's championships will be in Lexington, Kentucky, and I hope to attend it. I am also going to horse camps and riding lessons.

How did you get started in sports?

Jodelle: I have been riding horses since before I can remember. And before that my trainer, Joanne, would carry me around in a baby backpack while she gave my mom riding lessons. I joined Pony Club when I was five years old and am still in it.

Abigail: My mom has always had a passion for horses and rode when she was a kid up into her adulthood. So I think I got a lot of my love for horses from her. I'm pretty lucky to have a parent who's so into horses just like me. Now she couldn't get me out if she tried.

GIDDYUP, KIDDYUP!

Professional cowboys make the Pendleton Round-Up in Oregon a heart-pounding annual event. The Children's Rodeo offers children with special needs, mental or physical, the opportunity to be cowboys and cowgirls for an hour of horseback riding, steer roping, and barrel racing inside the Round-Up Arena.

What do you like best about sports?

Jodelle: I love competing on a team with my friends—we become closer and have a lot of fun. Plus, my horse is sort of like a therapist, keeping me sane. When I've had a bad day and I need to just forget it all, I ride. It gives my mind something else to think about and puts me in a better mood.

Abigail: I like building a relationship between the horse and me, getting to know what my horse likes and doesn't like. I also like how the sport teaches skills that I will be able to use in life, like teamwork and responsibility.

FAST FACT

Technology is a big part of sports. Scientists and corporations conduct research and experiments to design clothing, shoes, and equipment that allow athletes to break speed records and perform better.

Do you plan to stay in sports for a long time?

Jodelle: I plan to continue riding for the rest of my life. I think it's important to stay active, mentally and physically. Horses are a huge part of me, and if I just give them up, I would be giving up who I am.

Abigail: Yes, I do plan to stay in sports for a long time because I love riding and my horse. I plan to pass on riding to my kids, so they can enjoy it and pass it on to their kids. Riding is my life. I would go crazy if I couldn't ride.

What advice or tips can you give young people thinking of a career in sports?

Jodelle: Work at it, get connected, and be true to yourself. You won't be successful by just sitting around dreaming—you have to work toward what you want. Get connected with people who work in that career, find people who could be potential help when you are getting started. Don't go for it unless it's really what you want for yourself, not just what someone else wants for you.

Abigail: You have to love the sport and have a passion for it. If you don't love it, then you will be unhappy and might not stick with it. You have to give it your best, and if you don't enjoy what you are doing, then you won't give it your best.

A Passion for Coaching

Do you love watching others succeed—and knowing you helped them? Do you enjoy problem solving, planning, and leading? Maybe you don't have the chops to be a professional athlete in the big leagues—here or in Europe. That doesn't mean you still can't be part of a team. It takes an army of people to keep professional teams and athletes running. For every team, there is a coach—usually more than one. For example, professional baseball teams have hitting coaches and pitching coaches. All teams have strength and conditioning coaches who work with players to improve their speed, stamina, and other skills. Maybe your gift is helping others be great athletes by showing them how to play better. There's an old saying that no man is an island. Well, no athlete is an island either. Everyone needs support to be the best. And that means more jobs in sports—maybe one of which is just right for you!

Coaches aren't only needed at the professional level. There are probably dozens of coaches in your own hometown. Each high school and community team needs someone to lead it, to get the players to work as a team, to make sure each athlete performs to the best of his or her ability. Coaches have a big responsibility. Without a coach, teams and athletes could not function, and they wouldn't last very long. If you are good at

> Leadership, like coaching, is fighting for the hearts and souls of men and getting them to believe in you.
>
> **Eddie Robinson**
>
> CRICKETER

motivating people, at getting them to work together, at finding each athlete's strengths and helping that person develop them, then coaching could be an amazing way to work in the sports field.

Many coaches also double as teachers. You could be a physical education (PE) teacher in a school or community organization. This could be a great career if you like working with children, playing games, and helping young people have fun and stay healthy. Many coaches treasure the moments they share working with children and teenagers, and feel like they are shaping lives, not just athletes and teams. Or you could be a personal trainer, working with people who want to build healthier bodies. Perhaps you could start your own gym or exercise studio and train lots of people to stay physically fit.

Name: Vince Louther
Job: Athletic Coordinator, Clarkstown South High School, New City, New York

Why do you love sports?
They motivated me as a young person.

Why do you think it's important for young people to get involved in sports?
Involvement in sports teaches life lessons/skills.

What was your professional journey? How did you get to where you are today?
Collegiate sports led to physical education. My first teaching/coaching jobs led to lots of success and led me to believe I could do more for young people on a bigger stage.

What is a typical day like for you?
The day starts early and ends late with unanticipated challenges along the way.

What education did you pursue to get a job in this career? What classes were particularly helpful?
Physical/Health Education then Education Administration. The classes I took for my masters in counseling have been the most helpful when it comes to dealing with people.

What work or volunteer experiences helped you gain experience and contacts as you moved up in your career?
Several committee and community projects.

What is the best thing about your job?
Watching young people that I am familiar with compete.

What is the most challenging thing about your job?
Working with coaches, parents, and administration.

Who helped you the most in furthering your career and how?
A college professor/adviser had confidence in me to achieve more than I thought I could.

As a kid, did you think you would have this career when you grew up? Why or why not? What were your expectations?
I had no idea. I was living in the moment.

What advice or tips can you give young people thinking of a career in your field?
There is a solution to every challenge. If you cannot figure it out on your own, do not be embarrassed to ask for help.

Do you plan to stay in your career for a long time? If not, what do you think you will do after your career is over?
At least thirty years. I will get back into coaching, officiating, and enjoying hobbies.

What demands does your job put on your personal life? How do you deal with them?
It takes a lot of time. I deal with this by making the most of my time away from the job.

What is your salary or compensation?
To be honest, if you broke it down hourly, I would earn more working for McDonald's. What keeps me going is my love for the sport and the reactions I get when an athlete sees success. To me, that's what it's all about. In coaching and sports, you learn life lessons not just about a given sport.

A Passion for Calling the Shots

Do you love helping things run smoothly? Do you have good judgment, the ability to work well under pressure and make fast decisions, and a gift for resolving conflicts? Remember, athletes aren't the only ones on the playing field. What about referees, umpires, scorekeepers, linesmen, and other sports officials?

While many sports officials volunteer for local or regional events, some officials make it to the top of their game and work on major league events. They work their way up through the ranks, just like athletes do. Officiating can be a lucrative career. Believe it or not, a position as a top official is just as coveted as being the cleanup hitter or the starting quarterback. Imagine being a referee at the Super Bowl or an umpire at the World Series. What a thrill!

A Passion for Helping Others Feel Good

Do you enjoy staying off the field while still being connected to it? Are you fascinated with how the body works and how to keep it working at its best? Are you good at science and health classes? Just like athletes can't succeed without great coaching, they can't perform well if they are hurting. That's where sports medicine comes in.

You might be surprised at the number of career options there are in the field of sports medicine. Physical therapists and trainers help athletes recover from injuries and maximize performance through exercise and diet. Exercise physiologists study how the body works and how stress affects different body parts.

Sometimes it's a mental block that's keeping an athlete from doing his or her best. In that case, a sports psychologist will get into the athlete's mind to find ways to solve the problem and motivate the athlete to succeed. And of course, there are doctors, such as orthopedists, who specialize in treating sports-related injuries.

A Passion for the Business of Sports

Are you good at negotiating? Do you enjoy complimenting people and suggesting activities they'd be good at? Do you have a strong imagination and a great sense of fun? Maybe you're interested in the business side of sports. There are thousands of jobs managing teams, clubs, gyms, fitness centers, and other facilities.

The team's manager is responsible for getting athletes to play their best and win lots of games. Every team player signs a contract, so you could be a contracts manager, setting legal deals with new players on your team. Or you could be the agent who represents athletes and helps them get fair deals. Facility managers work at stadiums and other sporting venues, making sure the field is just right, the vendors are set up and ready to go, and everything is in place for the best fan experience. Talent scouts travel around the country, attending high school and college games, looking for hot, young players to sign. Then there are marketers, who promote teams and athletes and get the word out to the world about how great they are. A minor league team has to come up with fun promotions to keep the fans happy. All teams sell merchandise with their logos or names of their most famous players. Athletes do appearances to meet their fans and promote their team. All of these events are coordinated by the marketing department.

If you have a head for facts and figures or can see the big picture as you manage players and teams, a career in the business side of sports could be just right for you.

SPOTLIGHT

Tony Hawk: From Skateboarding Teen to Extreme Entrepreneur

When Tony Hawk was a kid growing up in San Diego, California, he was so hyperactive that his parents had him psychologically tested. It turned out that Hawk was super-smart—his IQ was 144—but needed plenty of stimulation to stay focused. Hawk's parents encouraged his interest in skateboarding as a way to burn off some energy, and the young teen thrived. He began going to competitions—and winning them. In 1982, when Hawk was just fourteen years old, he became a professional skateboarder. By the time he retired in 1999, he had become one of the most influential and well-known stars of extreme sports.

But Hawk's career was only just beginning. After he retired from competitions, he continued to be a big part of skateboarding. A video game series based on his skateboarding debuted in 1999 and became one of the most popular video games ever. Hawk also founded a YouTube channel called RIDE, licensed his name to shoes and clothing, and started a charitable foundation that has given away more than $3.4 million to build skateparks and help kids with economic disadvantages.

A Passion for Spreading the Word

Do you like to write? Do you want to be on television—but not sweaty on the court? Do you know how an f-stop affects the aperture? People wouldn't know about sports teams and athletes if no one talked about them. Sports broadcasting and other forms of journalism are exciting ways to get involved in sports.

MAKE THE CALL!

Play by Play Sports Broadcasting Camp is a five-day summer camp for kids ages ten to eighteen. Participants learn about being television, radio, and internet journalists, and many have gone on to impressive success. Here are just two examples: Sarah Barshop, who attended a camp in 2007, hosts a radio show at Marquette University and works for ESPN Radio Milwaukee. Daniel Radov attended the camp for eight years and, when he was seventeen years old, won a city-wide contest to host a weekly radio talk show on Baltimore's WNST. Camps happen in Atlanta, Baltimore, Boston, Chicago, Los Angeles, North Jersey, and Philadelphia.

There are all sorts of jobs for sports lovers in this field. You can be a sports reporter for a newspaper or a magazine. What about writing your own blog or website? If you want to do more research, write longer pieces, or study past sports accomplishments and failures consider being a sports historian. Fancy a career in broadcasting? Radio and television stations need reporters to go to games, interview athletes and managers, and describe all the highlights of the big game to audiences at home. Are you good with a camera? You might consider a career as a photographer, capturing those breathtaking moments of triumph and drama for people around the world to share.

CHECK IT OUT!

Are you amazed at the sheer number of career options available to you as a sports fan or player? Great! Then this is the book for you. In these pages, you'll find the secrets of career success in the sports world. You'll look at a variety of different job options and find out what each includes, what school classes will prepare you for that career, how to get experience outside of the classroom to train you for the job, and how to get your foot in the door and actually get a job in that career. Along the way, you'll meet and talk with lots of amazing people who have made sports their life, from coaches to managers, therapists to professional athletes, scouts to broadcasters. Before you take a fun quiz pointing out what sports career may be perfect for you, think some more about how long sports have been a part of human life.

FAST FACT

The first Olympic Games were held about 2,800 years ago in ancient Greece. Every four years, athletes would meet at Olympia. The first Olympics only had one footrace as an event. Later, other events were added, including boxing and discus throwing.

A LITTLE HISTORY . . .

When did organized sports start? No one knows the exact date, but it was definitely thousands of years ago. The first organized athletic events that we know a lot about are the Olympic Games, which were first held in ancient Greece way back in 776 BCE. These Olympics featured the greatest athletes from the Greek empire competing in footraces, throwing contests, and other events.

Though we don't know as much about other countries' and cultures' sporting events, we know they had them. The ancient Romans competed in chariot races and fight-to-the-death gladiator battles. Archaeologists found a stone ball and nine stone pins in an ancient Egyptian tomb, evidence of the sport we now call bowling. Lacrosse, one of today's fastest-growing youth sports, was originally played by Native Americans centuries ago. Soccer may be one of the oldest sports, probably dating back to ancient Asia. Of course, people have been skiing, skating, and probably knocking a rock or some other hard object across the ice for as long as there have been freezing winters and heavy snow.

Interest in sports in Europe grew during the Middle Ages. Tennis became popular with nobility during the 1200s. Golf and soccer also became popular in England. Horse racing, which was first organized during the Roman Empire, was an established sport in Europe by the late 1600s.

During the 1800s, sports that had been played casually became more organized. During this time, official rules were developed, as well as leagues and championships. The first modern track and field meet was held in England in 1825. Meanwhile, in the United States, the 1800s saw the first American college football game (Rutgers versus Princeton in 1869). Old British sports such as rounders and cricket developed into America's

> Most people never run far enough on their first wind to find out they've got a second.
>
> **William James**
>
> PHILOSOPHER AND PSYCHOLOGIST

pastime—baseball—in the mid-1800s. An American gym teacher invented basketball in 1891. Golf, tennis, boxing, competitive swimming, and many other sports gained in popularity during the late 1800s and beyond.

Athletic events have long been reported in newspapers and magazines and later on radio, television, and the Internet. The mid-1900s brought television to most American households, and that's when professional sports really took off. People could watch sporting events from the comfort of their own homes, miles away from where the events were taking place. Watching America's big four sports of the time—baseball, basketball, football, and hockey—became a nightly event in many homes, especially if the hometown team was in the championships. Other sports—everything from track and field to figure skating to auto racing—also attracted crowds at home and in the stands. Professional athletes became celebrities and figures to be admired by children and adults alike. Of course, amateur athletes got their due as well, especially if they played on college teams or were featured at the Olympics.

People weren't just watching sports during the twentieth century—they were taking part in them too! At least boys were—participating in Little League baseball, Pop Warner football, and many other team sports became a normal and expected part of many little boys' childhoods.

For centuries, girls did not participate in most sports at all. Tradition said that it was unattractive and unnatural for females to be athletic, and society certainly didn't consider participating in sports a feminine trait. Females slowly became part of certain sports, particularly golf, tennis, ice skating, swimming, and track and field. Girls did not have as many opportunities in sports until Title IX was passed in 1972. This landmark government legislation made it illegal to discriminate against females in sports and gave a lot more money to schools and community organizations in order to fund physical education and sports programs for girls. It also opened the door for girls to play Little League and other all-boy sports and, eventually, led to powerhouse women's teams in many college sports. Women also found more opportunities to play professional sports. The Women's National Basketball Association (WNBA) formed in 1997, and there are also professional women's teams in soccer, softball, and other sports.

The line between amateur and professional sports used to be crystal clear, but in recent years it has started to blur. The Olympics were once the high point of amateur athletics. Not only were none of the athletes who participated paid for going to the Olympics, but they weren't allowed to be paid for any athletic events or commercial endorsements even outside the Olympics. However, some countries paid for their athletes to train and compete, essentially making them professional athletes since they didn't have to work outside of sports for a living. Slowly, professional athletes from all over the world began to play in the Olympics. In 1992, one of the most talked-about teams in the Summer Games was the US men's basketball team, or the Dream Team, which featured basketball superstars from the NBA. The days of amateur-only Olympics were over.

> Never limit yourself, never be satisfied, and smile —it's free!
>
> **Jennie Finch**
> SOFTBALL PLAYER

The worldwide love of sports has made becoming a professional athlete a dream for many young people. However, the harsh reality is that most kids who are really good at sports will never achieve the high-profile status of major league stars. Still, there's nothing wrong with a dream, and there's no harm in knowing how to make the most of your chances if you want to be a professional athlete.

Score! A Sports Career Quiz

Take this quiz and see what sports career could be the best fit for you.

1. My favorite subject in school is
   A. English
   B. Math
   C. Science
   D. Gym
   E. Psychology
   F. History

2. In my neighborhood, I'm known as the kid who can
   A. Write a prize-winning essay or story
   B. Work a deal to put money in my pocket
   C. Help fix injuries
   D. Win any sports competition, hands down
   E. Help others do better at anything they try
   F. Rattle off facts and statistics about my favorite sport

3. In my spare time, I like to hang out in
   A. The library
   B. The school store
   C. The science lab
   D. The gym
   E. The homework help center
   F. The museum

4. My idea of a great birthday present is
   A. A flashy digital camera or computer
   B. Money to invest in the stock market
   C. An illustrated guide to the human body
   D. A new piece of sports equipment

E. A chance to play with younger kids

F. An artifact from a historical event

5. When I watch a game on television, I wonder

A. What questions the press will ask the players after the game

B. How much money the athletes are making

C. If the trainers iced the athlete's sore arm before the game

D. What exciting plays I'll see

E. If each player is being treated fairly

F. If something memorable or historic will happen

6. At a neighborhood or school sporting event, I'm most likely to be

A. Writing notes for the school paper

B. Selling refreshments in the stands

C. Helping the coach tape up the players' ankles

D. Right in the thick of the game

E. Encouraging the athletes to do their best

F. Trying to catch a ball thrown into the stands

FAST FACT

Early Olympics included some events we'd consider odd today, such as ballooning, obstacle-race swimming, and pole climbing.

7. I'd like a job where I can

A. Make my own hours and be creative

B. Tell other people what to do and keep everything organized

C. Help people feel well and not get injured or sick

D. Be active and travel a lot

E. Help other people be great at what they do

F. Be around things that change the world

If you answered mostly A's, you'd probably be great at a career in media, whether it's broadcasting or announcing a game, writing articles or books, or taking photographs.

If you answered mostly B's, think about a career in management, business, or agenting.

If you answered mostly C's, you should explore a career in sports medicine, fitness training, or personal training.

If you answered mostly D's, you'd be happiest playing sports for a living.

If you answered mostly E's, you have a great personality for coaching or teaching.

If you answered mostly F's, you would probably enjoy a career as an archivist or sports historian.

Now that you have an idea what you might like to do, it's time to explore all your options and see how to steer your life where you want it to go. On your mark, get set, *go*!

2

Keep Your Eye on the Ball: Sports Players

THE CREAM OF THE CROP

Becoming a professional major league athlete is a long shot. Just look at the numbers. While there are thousands of college, high school, and community teams that compete on the amateur level, there are far fewer professional sports teams.

Of course, not all athletes play on teams. There are tennis players, golfers, swimmers, ice skaters, and many others who compete individually. However, when these athletes compete in tournaments, only the top few finishers are paid the big bucks, leaving it impossible for lower-ranking athletes to train and compete full-time and still be able to afford a place to live and to put food on the table.

How many professional major league teams are in the United States?

National Football League (NFL): 32

Major League Baseball (MLB): 30

National Basketball Association (NBA): 30

National Hockey League (NHL): 30

Major League Soccer (MLS): 19

Women's National Basketball Association (WNBA): 12

Compare these numbers to about two hundred Division I college football teams alone. There simply is no space for most college athletes—even really good athletes—in the majors.

In addition, not all athletes who play professionally can do it for a long time. Injuries and age knock many strong athletes out of the major leagues and back into the "regular" world.

Train, Train, Train

Anyone who wants to be a professional athlete better be willing to work hard. The key to getting noticed and advancing in a sport is to win competitions. An athlete who doesn't train has about as much chance of winning as a hamster racing against a herd of gazelles. Athletes need skill, but they also need stamina, flexibility, and strength. Training is the best way to accomplish this.

Athletes train all year, not just during the playing season. Training includes stretching and exercising the specific muscles used in a particular

It is not the size of the man but the size of his heart that matters.

Evander Holyfield

BOXER

sport, as well as working with weights to build muscle strength and cardio to improve stamina and endurance. Athletes don't want just to stay in top condition during the off-season—you want to improve every part of your performance. To do this, an athlete will work on specific muscle groups or skills. For example, a figure skater might practice jumps and spins, while a tennis player might hit hundreds of balls over the net to perfect forehand shots.

Training is not an activity the athlete does alone. Coaches, trainers, teammates, and even friends train with the athlete, helping you do better and encouraging you not to give up. In addition, athletes often videotape workouts and then watch the tapes to see where they could do better. Even the slightest change can make a big difference in performance.

What's the point of mentioning all this training? It's just to let any potential superstar know that being a professional athlete is not all fun and games. It's hard work!

Names: Sisters Claire and Lydia Tembreull (with their mom, Ann, who has her own profile on being a swim official in chapter 5)
Ages: 13 and 10
Job (when not studying!): Swimmers, Northern Lights Swim Team, Escanaba, Michigan

What sports have you participated in and when?
Claire: Swimming since I was a baby.
Lydia: I've been on the swim team since I was five years old.

What are you doing now in terms of education/sports participation?

Claire: I go to practice three times a week for an hour and a half during the regular swim season, which runs from October to March. I also swim on the summer swim team, which works on technique.

Lydia: Like Claire, I go to practice three times a week for an hour and a half during the regular swim season from October to March. I also swim on the summer swim team, which works on technique.

Ann: Just this past year, our school district formed a high school swim team. It is a satellite program of our Y, which makes things convenient. It will be another nice option for our kids when they reach high school age. Girls who swim are much sought after for college programs. We have seen several girls who have done very well on the team and been offered nice scholarships even if they don't swim on the A team at college. It does make staying on the team attractive for their future, but hopefully that isn't the only reason to be there.

How did you get started in sports?

Claire: I've taken swim lessons since I was fourteen months old, and I joined the swim team when I was six.

Lydia: I started taking swim lessons when I was thirteen months old, and I joined the swim team when I was five years old.

FAST FACT

The 1908 Olympics were the first to have a swimming pool. Before then, Olympic swimmers competed in the ocean or in rivers.

Ann: I have always loved to swim and encouraging my kids to swim became a physical necessity when Claire started walking and developed problems with her legs. We ended up at Children's Hospital of Wisconsin in Milwaukee, where a geneticist told us Claire was super flexible and prone to sprains. His

24

suggestion to strengthen her legs: swimming! We've pretty much been fixtures at the YMCA ever since.

I really never thought we'd be involved so deeply in a competitive sport. Claire went from the minnow level of swimming lessons to swim team at age six. She was so nervous at her first meet. She ended up receiving a heat winner ribbon, and that was all it took for her to be hooked.

> Make sure your worst enemy doesn't live between your own two ears.
>
> **Laird Hamilton**
> SURFER

Lydia ended up on the swim team after watching Claire swim during a summer practice. One of the coaches asked if she wanted to try it, and she did. She swam her first relay about a week later in a dual meet on a team with the head coach's high-school-senior son, who was 6'3". The contrast of tall Zach and tiny Lydia was priceless. It's one of our funniest swim team moments.

What do you like best about sports?
Claire: I love hanging out with my friends and cheering for them. I love swimming!
Lydia: I love to just hang out with my friends and try to beat my own time. I also like to cheer for the team.
Ann: One thing we really like about swimming is that even if you don't place in the top three in your race, you often score points for the team as a whole. Not only are there the individual awards but a team award as well. We can often say to our kids that they helped the team win the meet. We try to encourage our kids to set goals and try their best. In our family, it's nice to be first, but it's also great to participate.

Do you plan to stay in sports for a long time?
Claire: Yes, because I love swimming, I will try to continue down the road.

Lydia: I think sports will always be a part of my life because I think swimming is so much fun. I will continue to swim.

Ann: What I hoped they would get out of swimming was a lifelong physical activity. There really aren't that many sports that you play as a kid that can follow you no matter your age or physical limitations. Plus, living on Lake Michigan, it is so important to have a respect for the water and the lake. I hope that even if both girls decide to stop swimming competitively, they will always enjoy swimming for fun. If that happens, my goal has been achieved.

What advice or tips can you give young people thinking of a career in sports?

Claire: Go for it and don't worry about messing up or not winning. Go and cheer for your team and be the best you can be.

Lydia: The advice I would give is just have fun and don't worry if you don't win because you can always try again next time. I would also tell you to try your hardest.

The Path to the Pros

So you're ready to accept the challenges and hard work. You think you can beat the odds and make it to the pros in your particular sport. Good for you! The question you're probably wondering now is: How do I start?

It seems obvious to say this, but the best way to start is to play the sport you love. Most athletes who turn pro have been playing since they were little kids. Did Derek Jeter play Little League? You bet he did. Was Mia Hamm kicking a soccer ball when she was barely out of preschool? You know it. Most athletes didn't just start playing when they were little—they also showed a great aptitude. This is especially true of athletes who participate in individual sports, such as gymnastics and tennis. In these sports, high school students can become internationally known stars and receive lots of money, either for winning competitions or for endorsing products. They don't need to wait until they are fully grown up to turn professional.

For team players, being on a high school team is especially important. Talent scouts hear about the best high school players, and they are eager to see what these players can do. A good athlete might be noticed by a professional sports team and be drafted into the organization's minor league system. However, it's more likely that the athlete will attract the notice of college scouts. This can be a very good thing. Many athletes receive hefty scholarships—sometimes the cost of their entire college education—just to play on a school's team. And for many sports, especially football and basketball, a great college playing career is the way to get noticed by the professional teams. It's no accident that the top draft picks in the NBA and NFL are almost always key players on college teams. It's a win-win situation—a free or low-cost education at a top school, a chance to play your favorite sport, and the possibility of being noticed and drafted by a pro team.

Going to college is a plus in many other ways besides providing the opportunity to maybe play pro sports. Even if you are lucky enough to have a pro career, the odds are that you won't be playing in the big leagues for more than a few years. That means that you'll have to find another job. Having a college degree can prepare you for that day. In addition, college courses in accounting, business, law, marketing, or medicine can help you handle the challenges and opportunities that will come up during your sports career.

A pro athlete has to have a very special personality. You have to have unbelievable levels of determination. Giving up, taking a day

> **FAST FACT**
>
> During the 1896 Olympic swimming competition, conditions were so rough that gold medalist Alfréd Hajós said, "My will to live completely overcame my desire to win!"

off, or quitting because you are tired or sore or frustrated is simply not an option. If you want to be a professional athlete, you have to be 100 percent committed to succeeding, and you must work nonstop to improve your skills, do your best, and get noticed so you can move up to the next level. Self-confidence and ambition are key aspects that are almost as important as raw athletic ability. As a baseball scout commented to a player, "Attitude is everything! Act like you own the place. When you walk off the field, hold your head high and act like you're a star. That confidence will get you noticed and improve your game."[1]

Sportsmanship is also important. You don't want to be the piece that doesn't fit. You don't want to be the guy or girl who your teammates groan about or who leaves a sour taste in everyone's mouth. Good sportsmanship is not only a good personal quality to have— but it can also make you money. Sponsors don't like athletes who get into trouble or act like bullies or whiners. The big endorsement deals and the fat contracts aren't going to go to the athletes who get in trouble with the law or who have scandal and bad news following their every step. Ability + determination + class = success!

A Cautionary Tale

In 2003, eighteen-year-old Eric Duncan was a first-round draft pick for the New York Yankees. The shortstop was a power hitter with a strong work ethic. During a workout at Yankee Stadium before the draft, scouts saw Duncan hit home runs into the second deck. The scouts reported that Duncan was the most exciting player they'd seen. He was focused, prepared, mature, and ready for the big time.

Most pro sports—football, hockey, basketball, and soccer—draft their players out of college and have them play in developmental leagues before moving up to the big time. However, baseball is unique in that it has an established system of minor league teams (also called farm teams). Players usually start at the lowest level, which is called A, and, if they're lucky, advance to AA and then AAA. The next stop is the Major Leagues.

SPORTS IN THE MOVIES

Sports movies have been popular ever since movies began! Here are some highlights through the years:

1942 *The Pride of the Yankees* (baseball)

1944 *National Velvet* (horse racing)

1949 *Take Me Out to the Ball Game* (baseball)

1951 *Angels in the Outfield* (baseball)

1975 *The Other Side of the Mountain* (skiing)

1976 *Rocky* (boxing)

1978 *Ice Castles* (figure skating)

1979 *Breaking Away* (cycling)

1979 *The Black Stallion* (horse racing)

1981 *Chariots of Fire* (track)

1984 *The Natural* (baseball)

1984 *The Karate Kid* (martial arts)

1986 *Hoosiers* (basketball)

1988 *Eight Men Out* (baseball)

1989 *Field of Dreams* (baseball)

1989 *Major League* (baseball)

1992 *A League of Their Own* (baseball)

1992 *The Cutting Edge* (figure skating)

1992 *The Mighty Ducks* (hockey)

1993 *Cool Runnings* (bobsled)

1993 *Rookie of the Year* (baseball)

1993 *Rudy* (football)

1994 *Angels in the Outfield* (remake) (baseball)

1994 *Hoop Dreams* (basketball)

1996 *Space Jam* (basketball)

2000 *Legend of Bagger Vance* (golf)

2002 *The Rookie* (baseball)

2002 *Blue Crush* (surfing)

2003 *Seabiscuit* (horse racing)

2004 *Miracle* (ice hockey)

2004 *Mr. 3000* (baseball)

2004 *Wimbledon* (tennis)

2005 *Cinderella Man* (boxing)

2008 *Sticks and Stones* (hockey)

2009 *The Blind Side* (football)

2009 *Whip It* (roller derby)

2010 *Secretariat* (horse racing)

2010 *The Karate Kid* (remake) (martial arts)

2011 *Moneyball* (baseball)

2011 *Soul Surfer* (surfing)

2012 *Crooked Arrows* (lacrosse)

2012 *Trouble with the Curve* (baseball)

2013 *42* (baseball)

2013 *Drift* (surfing)

After joining the Yankees organization, Duncan moved quickly through the lower levels of the minor leagues. Surely it was only a matter of time before he made it to the major leagues. But, as a news reporter later wrote, "A baseball contract offers no promises. Not for the organization. Not for the player."[2]

Eric Duncan played for the Yankees minor league team until 2009. Then he went to the Kansas City Royals and played in its minor-league system until 2012. Over his ten-year career, Duncan had almost four thousand times at bat, but he never made even one appearance in the Major Leagues. After the 2012 season ended, Duncan quit baseball and enrolled in college at the age of twenty-eight.

What happened? Many factors combined to stop Duncan's climb into the majors. His hits and at bats declined. He had trouble hitting curveballs. Then doctors discovered a vision problem that made it hard for Duncan to see the ball under the lights during night games. Slowly, Duncan lost his confidence and left professional sports, telling people that he didn't want to end up resenting the game he loved so much.

Duncan's story is not uncommon. Most of the players who are drafted by major league teams never play in the major leagues or play only a few games. A player might spend his whole career in the minors, or he might only play a few seasons. As long as you understand this and play for the love of the game, you can enjoy your time as a professional athlete. But if you enter the draft feeling that being a big-shot player is the only way to succeed, odds are you will be very disappointed.

SPOTLIGHT

Jeremy Lin: Most Unexpected American to Play a Great American Game

Jeremy Lin is the first American of Taiwanese or Chinese descent (he's both) to play on an NBA team. But even outside of that, it's pretty amazing that in 2012, he signed a three-year contract with the Houston Rockets. He made it to professional basketball without a college athletic scholarship, without being drafted right after college graduation and after being sent multiple times to the D-League, the NBA Development League.

Though Lin inspired a fan frenzy dubbed Linsanity after he became a starter for the New York Knicks, his first NBA team, Lin prefers to lead his life as plainly as he can. He earned a degree in economics from Harvard University, slept on couches in his brother's and a teammate's apartments even after joining the NBA, and has said he'd like to become a pastor after his professional basketball days are over.

Show Me the Money

How much can a pro athlete make? The sky's the limit when it comes to the very best in the game—we've all heard about the multimillion-dollar contracts commanded by the superstars of baseball, basketball, football, and other major sports, and the fat endorsement deals snatched up by Olympic champions and other sports heroes. However, not everyone is making that kind of money. For every top athlete who earns millions of dollars a year, there are hundreds of athletes earning a "regular" person's salary. But those hundreds of lesser-paid athletes are still being paid to play the sport they love, and that is not a bad thing!

LIFE IN THE MINORS

Many farm teams are associated with Major League teams, but there are also independent baseball leagues that are not affiliated with specific teams. Players in these leagues do have the opportunity to be seen by Major League scouts, however. Many of the players in the independent leagues are college age or older and just enjoy playing baseball. Most minor league seasons last from late May or early June until Labor Day.

> The five S's of sports training are: stamina, speed, strength, skill, and spirit, but the greatest of these is spirit.
>
> **Ken Doherty**
>
> SNOOKER PLAYER

Life in the minor leagues is far from glamorous. Most do not make enough to live on their own, and the league will set you up with host families who charge very little for room and board. During the off-season, some of the players will go to Puerto Rico or Central or South America to play winter ball. It isn't the money that drives you—it's the love of the game.

Name: Danielle DeStaso
Age: 20
Job (when not studying!): Pitcher, softball, Seton Hall University, New Jersey
Dream Job: Coach

Why do you think it's important for young people to get involved in sports?
In high school I played softball and basketball. I've always been a part of sports. I love the family you get out if it. The friends I make through it are ones that are always there, and they become family because of the time and work you put into it together. I also enjoy sports because they are fun and they provide something to keep me going.

Do you plan to stay in sports for a long time?
I know sports will always be a part of my life. I'd love to play professional softball, but there isn't a good league for that, so after college I don't know where I will play. What I'd really love is to coach in a high school. I want to teach children to love something as much as I do.

What advice or tips can you give young people thinking of a career in sports?

Teenagers looking to continue in sports need to be willing to work hard. It is definitely a lot of fun, but they have to realize what comes with it, especially in college. They will have to learn to make sacrifices if they want to be the best. In the end, their hard work will pay off and they will learn to love what they do, just like I do!

Notes:

1. John Burns, conversation with author, March 18, 2013.

2. Chad Jennings, "He Looked the Part," *The Journal News* (February 10, 2013): 1C.

3

A Guiding Hand: Coaches and Teachers

It's fair to say that no great athlete ever got to the top of his or her field without a few coaches helping along the way. Often a coach or a PE teacher is the first person to help athletes discover their skills and develop them to their full potential. Even if a player doesn't become a professional athlete, that person can thank a coach for teaching important life lessons. Do you have what it takes to become a coach or a PE teacher?

ONE JOB, MANY RESPONSIBILITIES

Coaches work with a team or with individuals. Your job is to teach athletes the skills they need to succeed. In the case of a team

9 QUALITIES GOOD COACHES HAVE

1. Patience
2. Optimism
3. Discipline
4. Knowledge
5. Understanding
6. Determination
7. Motivation
8. Communication
9. Encouragement

coach, you are also responsible for getting the players to work together as a unit. Coaches work with players regularly, sometimes every day in the case of those on a school team during the season. You are also present during competitions, guiding players.

Many coaches work for schools. In addition to coaching a sport after school, most school coaches also work as teachers. While some teach subjects such as social studies or math, others make sports part of the teaching job as well. A PE teacher spends the day introducing children to games and sports. The goal is to teach children healthy habits and get them to become active. Working as a PE teacher and a coach is a perfect blend.

Coaches are also responsible for safety. Coaches and teachers need to make sure students have the right equipment and know how to use it correctly. Coaches also stress safety by teaching students how to play confidently, follow the rules, and use the correct techniques when playing a sport.

Motivation is another big part of coaching and teaching. Some students may enjoy playing but not be willing to put in the hard work they need to do to succeed. A good coach or teacher motivates students to go beyond what they expected in order to achieve their best. As most coaches say, physical training isn't the only part of being an athlete; psychological training is important too. With motivation comes discipline. Coaches have the tough but rewarding job of instilling discipline in students. Why else would athletes do drills and exercises over and over again, even in bad weather or when they're already exhausted after a long day at school?

profile

Name: Kristof Schroeder
Age: 21
Job (when not studying!): Football player, recent graduate of the University of Puget Sound, Washington
Dream Job: Future coach

What sports have you participated in and when?
When I was in the fifth grade, I began playing organized basketball at my middle school. We played against the other Catholic schools' teams in the Portland, Oregon, metropolitan area. The teams I played on were successful, for the most part. However, I really wanted to play football. My parents didn't let me play until high school. I started playing my freshman year. Because I was busy juggling football and my musical endeavors, I stopped playing basketball. In the spring, I started track and field. I ran the 400 meter dash, but I wasn't very good, and I wasn't enjoying it, so I started throwing the javelin. I improved greatly at the event, and I continued to throw until my senior year. I also continued with football, and I lettered twice, in my junior and senior years. I was also a member of my conference's all-conference team my senior year as a first-team member. I continued playing football at the collegiate level. I have also played one season in Austria,

> Gold medals aren't really made of gold. They're made of sweat, determination, and a hard-to-find alloy called guts.
>
> **Dan Gable**
>
> AMATEUR WRESTLER AND COACH

with the Salzburg Bulls, and I will play this summer in Finland for the Kouvola Indians.

What are you doing now in terms of education/sports participation?

I just finished my collegiate career. At the moment, I am training and getting ready for my season abroad in Finland.

How did you get started in sports?

I got started in sports when I was very young. My father always taught me about football, basketball, and baseball. I guess you could say I was bound to start playing at some point.

What do you like best about sports?

I am a *huge* fan of the competitive nature of sports. There's nothing better than watching a football team march down the field to avoid going to overtime and scoring the game-winning touchdown or watching two great basketball teams duking it out until the final buzzer. In terms of actually playing, it's great when, no matter the result of the contest, I can look my teammates and coaches right in the eye and be able to say I gave my all for them. Competition is great.

Do you plan to stay in sports for a long time?

I am very sure that sports will always be a part of my life. This coming football season in Finland will most likely be my last season as a player, as I feel there's not a whole lot more I can do on the field as a player. I can do a lot as a coach however. I will always want to coach, whether it is at the high school, college, or professional level.

FAST FACT

Starting blocks were first used at the 1928 Olympics to prevent runners from slipping when they started. Today, starting blocks have a device that can tell if an athlete starts before the starting gun goes off.

What are your career goals and dreams?

Assuming I am able to coach, I want to give my players the same feeling I got when I stepped on the field, especially when I was part of a winning program. There's no greater feeling than knowing you are completely prepared to play against an opponent. I want that feeling to drive my players and get them to a championship level. Through their hard work that I will push them to do, I want them to feel as if they are unstoppable. But being unstoppable means that the players have to have a humble attitude. A team can't be cocky. It's kind of like the Teddy Roosevelt quote: "Speak softly, and carry a big stick."

What advice or tips can you give young people thinking of a career in sports?

I would tell young people to listen to their coaches. No matter how respected or hated a coach might be, that person is always providing some sort of learning experiences. Some of the best lessons and motivation came from the worst coaches I ever had. A good coach sets a great foundation for a future coach (or person in another athletic-related career). Then one can build on that foundation. Lessons learned indirectly from a bad or less-respected coach can be used in order to determine what not to do in the future. It's really important to pay attention to your coaches.

Please describe your experiences playing and coaching in Europe. How is the sports scene there different than it is in the United States?

Playing in Europe was definitely one of the greatest experiences I have ever had. I made many new friends along the way. Playing there is definitely completely different than it is here. There isn't as much of an emphasis on sports in Europe as there is here in America. Still, those who are involved are very passionate about what they do, especially the die-hard American-football guys. The speed of the game is a lot slower than in America, and at times, it was hard to get all the guys at practice, even though practice was only twice a week. Football is a club sport over there. That means the guys have to pay for their own equipment, which is expensive. They don't get paid anything, and teams rely heavily on commercial sponsors. Still, the players are passionate about the game, and they probably love it more than we do over here. There's a great environment for football over there, and it's slowly starting to build. There is great potential for football to become a major sport in the European athletic scene.

Training to Coach and Teach

People who want to coach, especially in a school environment, need to follow a specific area of study. Most school coaches have at least a bachelor's degree, usually in education or in the specific subject you want to teach. In addition, many coaches and teachers have master's degrees in coaching, counseling, education, or psychology. Teachers need to be certified, and many places require coaches to be certified too. Each state has different certification requirements. You can get information from your guidance counselor or career counselor or from the teachers you have when you go to college.

To prepare for college and a coaching or teaching career, high school students should

GET ON THE ROAD

to a Coaching Career by Getting a Paid or Volunteer Job with

- School teams
- Local teams
- Camps
- Youth leagues
- Gyms
- Recreation centers
- YMCA or other community organizations

take health courses as well as science courses, such as biology and anatomy, in order to learn about the human body. English and speech courses are also important, since a big part of coaching and teaching is communicating with students. Participation in gym class and after-school sports is a huge plus. Along with studying, you can gain valuable coaching experience by volunteering or helping out local teams.

The Green off the Field

There is a wide variety of salaries in the coaching and teaching professions. Someone who is coaching an Olympic athlete or a major league team is making a lot more money than someone coaching a youth league basketball team or a swimming class at the YMCA. Many teachers receive a salary for teaching along with extra pay for coaching at the school. As one of our profiled teacher-coaches, Tony Mellino, whom you'll hear more from soon, said, his annual salary "sounds good per hour, but for all the time I put in, it probably amounts to about fifty-eight cents per hour!"

Name: Joseph Lofberg
Job: PE teacher, R. P. Connor Elementary School, Suffern, New York

Why do you love sports?
I love sports for many reasons. It has provided me many opportunities and life lessons. Here are just a few things I love about sports:

1. Teamwork
2. Leadership
3. Hard work/the payoff
4. Disappointment/leaving you wanting more
5. Sports allows me to dream big
6. Pride/ownership in something
7. Accountability

Why do you think it's important for young people to get involved in sports?
I feel it's important for children to get involved in sports for the exercise as well as for the competition itself. It's important for children to learn how to win and to lose. Sports provide young people the importance of teamwork, leadership, and how to work hard. In sports, you are accountable for your mistakes.

What is a typical day like for you?
I wake up about 6:00 AM and help my wife get our kids ready for the day. My wife is a teacher as well, so we have to drop the kids off at day care before we go off to work. I teach morning gym class for an hour before school starts, and then I work my normal class schedule throughout the day. After school I go off to coach ice hockey at night. I typically get home about 6:30 PM.

What education did you pursue to get a job in this career?
At the State University of New York at Oswego, communications with a minor in coaching. At Montclair State University in New Jersey, master's in education.

What work or volunteer experiences helped you gain experience and contacts as you moved up in your career?
I'm a big believer in giving back. I've done volunteer work with the Reach Foundation of Suffern, which provides

educational funding for schools, as well as for the Suffern Ice Hockey Program and the Christmas toy drive sponsored by the local police department's DARE unit. These experiences helped me to give back to the town and to work with people who have a passion for what they do. I really believe that the pleasure of volunteering and helping others and meeting such wonderful people helped me to move up in my career.

What's the best thing about your job?
Kids always come into school or my class with a smile, which in return makes me smile.

What's the most challenging thing about your job?
The most challenging thing about my job is making sure that each kid is engaged. Each lesson needs to be geared toward all the kids in the hopes that they take something away from the lesson.

What sports did you play as a kid?
Many sports, including ice hockey, baseball, lacrosse, and soccer.

What advice or tips can you give young people thinking of a career in your field?
Do what you love and don't settle. I love kids and sports, and as a PE teacher I get to work with kids and teach what I love. Also, it's important to educate yourself not only in the classroom but through real-life experiences.

Do you plan to stay in your career for a long time? If not, what do you think you will do after your career is over?
I plan on being a PE teacher for my

This ability to conquer oneself is no doubt the most precious of all things sports bestows.

Olga Korbut

GYMNAST

whole career. I have a love for it and don't see myself doing any other job.

What demands does your job put on your personal life? How do you deal with them?
There isn't enough time to fit everything I have to do into one day, and my job also takes away time I can be with my family.

FROM PLAYER TO COACH

Even major league ballplayers want to be coaches. For twenty-three years, Omar Vizquel played shortstop in the major leagues. He was a terrific player, racking up eleven Gold Gloves (a prestigious fielding award) and earning a .985 fielding percentage—the best fielding percentage by a shortstop in major league history. When Vizquel retired in October 2012, many people expected him to go home to Seattle and spend time enjoying his hobbies, which include painting, sculpting, and photography. Instead, Vizquel became a minor league infield instructor for the California Angels. His job: to teach the fine points of fielding to new players.

Vizquel relishes his new role. He sees it as a stepping stone on his way to possibly managing a team someday. Most of all, Vizquel enjoys helping younger players and being around his beloved game of baseball. "The baseball world is the best work that a man can have," he said. As for being a coach, "I think it's awesome. I think it's just like going back to high school, when you had to be a teacher or a leader and a good role

> We're prepared, and we've done everything we can to prepare for this moment in time. That's what confidence is all about.
>
> **Lisa Fernandez**
>
> SOFTBALL PLAYER AND COACH

model for them. You are there for them to help them out. I love to teach. I love to pass my knowledge to other people, so maybe they can be a solid major league player someday. I think that would be the greatest satisfaction."[1]

Name: Tony Mellino
Job: Varsity wrestling coach, Clarkstown High School North, New City, New York

Why do you love sports?
I love the duality of both the internal drive athletes possess individually and how this personal goal setting needs to meld within a team framework in order for all to find success. A team is only as strong as its weakest link. We always preach to our team that you don't deserve anything from sports, but you get what you earn. We also tell them that sports does not build character but rather reveals character.

Why do you think it's important for young people to get involved in sports?
Goal setting and what it will take to achieve this goal; facing adversity and learning from it; dealing with setbacks that should make you stronger rather than knock you down; handling success with humility and defeat with pride; perseverance when you want to quit; and refocusing your goals once they are met. These are not sports lessons but life lessons, and that is why it is so important for young people to get involved in sports today. My father uses a funny analogy with

our athletes. He tells them competing in sports is like taking a trip to Oz. Some will need to find courage in order to compete, some will need brains and have to better use their intelligence, and others will need heart, so when the time comes, they don't wither under the intensity. If each athlete can figure out what is missing, it will be a life lesson as well as a sports lesson.

What was your professional journey? How did you get to where you are today?
I grew up around sports all my life. My father taught high school social studies for forty years and was a high school wrestling coach for forty years, a freshman/JV [junior varsity] soccer coach for thirty-eight years, and a lacrosse/baseball coach for thirty-six years. My mother was also the secretary to our district's athletic director, so my earliest memories are of many days spent around athletic facilities. When it was time to figure out what I wanted to do with my life after receiving a bachelor's degree in history from Binghamton University, I decided to pursue education and got my master's degree in elementary education from Hofstra University. Two months later, I was hired to teach in the Clarkstown Central School District. The very day I was hired, I stopped by the athletic office to let them know of my interest in coaching, and as fate would have it, their assistant wrestling coach had resigned that morning. That was twenty-one years ago, and I have been coaching wrestling here ever since, the past seventeen as a varsity coach. I also have coached modified soccer for seventeen seasons and coached four seasons of modified baseball as well.

> **FAST FACT**
>
> The first voice broadcast of a sporting event took place on April 11, 1921, when radio station KDKA in Pittsburgh, Pennsylvania, broadcast a boxing match between Johnny Dundee and Johnny Ray at Pittsburgh's Motor Square Garden.

MODIFIED SPORTS[2]

According to New York State, a modified sports program includes the following standards:

It is extremely important that ALL students involved at this level on the interscholastic program have a positive, meaningful, and productive experience. It is also important that ALL students have reasonable opportunity to test learned skills in a competitive situation, and that such competition be as equitable as possible.

THE PHILOSOPHY OF MODIFIED SPORTS:

1. To provide as broad and varied an athletic program as is possible with an opportunity for competition on an equal basis for all students. A desirable program will encourage participation in intramural competition at several achievement levels and provide interschool competition in a modified sports program for the more talented in as large a variety of sports as possible.

2. To realize that the individual schools have the final responsibility to equalize competition and must administer the program so that no overmatching of teams or individuals shall be permitted.

3. To conduct the athletic program so that educational objectives shall be achieved; so that the highest ideals of sportsmanship are upheld; so that no single phase of the educational program is promoted at the expense of other equally important programs.

4. To realize that the athletic programs must be integrated with all other activities essential to youth, including those that may be conducted by out-of-school groups, to avoid an excessive load for any student.

5. To administer the program in such a manner that participants are properly examined, approved, equipped, insured, selected, classified, instructed, and supervised so that as safe a program as is possible is conducted.

6. To administer the program so that there shall be no over-emphasis, minimum loss of school time, with limited publicity, competent officiating, limited awards (for example, paper certificates, ribbons) and all efforts made to keep in a proper perspective.

7. To provide qualified faculty leadership that understands the teaching of sports to the age group, the objectives of this modified sports program, and the emphasis of safety procedures.

8. To cooperate with schools in the area in providing an inter-school athletic administrative unit that will achieve the objectives and will aid in the development of the highest type of cordial interschool relationships.

9. To conduct the program so that the proper respect for authority is achieved and so that all evidences of undesirable athletic mannerisms are avoided.

10. To compete within the spirit of the rules, to give every opponent due credit and respect, and to win honorably and lose graciously.

11. To finance the program through the Board of Education approved funds.

12. To cooperate with the Sectional Athletic Council in its efforts to provide sound leadership for all junior high schools in the section. No league or sectional team or individual championships are to be conducted.

What is a typical day like for you?

During wrestling season, it is extraordinarily busy! I usually get to the school two hours before the opening bell, when I first check my email to see what communications I have received from my athletic director, the Section I wrestling chairman, and colleagues asking me questions about the NWCA Database for which I have become an unofficial expert on using. [This database is a computer system for inputting results and record keeping, and it is mandatory for all New York State wrestling coaches.]

I then plan out my practice for the day. The time that remains is for prepping for my day's social studies lessons and giving extra help to my students. I then teach grade six social studies throughout the day. During off periods, I may peruse results, update records, and if I have time, grab a quick lunch. After I am done there, I get to the high school by 2:50 PM or so for practice, which goes until about 5:30 PM. After practice, I mop/disinfect the wrestling mats, clean the locker room, inventory my medical kit, and then finally get home about twelve to thirteen hours after I left.

On nine consecutive Saturdays this season, we had wrestling tournaments. This involves getting on a bus in the early hours, as early as 5:30 AM but never later than 6:30. We then get to the site, have weigh-ins, and then the tournament begins. This tournament will take all day, and I usually do not return back to the high school until well after 9:00 at night—I have gotten home past midnight.

What education did you pursue to get a job in this career? What classes were particularly helpful?
Along with the bachelor's degree in history from Binghamton University, a master's in elementary education from Hofstra University and sixty postgraduate credits in education, I have also taken some coaching courses on philosophy of coaching, theory and technique of coaching, and coaching practicums, which were mandated by New York State. Since I began coaching, I've also had to take a biyearly CPR/AED [cardiopulmonary resuscitation/automated external defibrillator] course, a first aid course and update, and a heat clinic course [which helps train coaches in how to avoid illness when practicing in hot temperatures].

As a new coach, I was fortunate to take some of my earliest courses with an athletic director from another school. This was a fantastic opportunity to learn the ins and outs of coaching, from the simplest and most mundane tasks to the more complicated coach-player and coach-parent relationships. His insight was invaluable.

What work or volunteer experiences helped you gain experience and contacts as you moved up in your career?

I got to know my fellow coaches, built a strong relationship with our Section I chairman, and am now the vice president of wrestling for Rockland County as well as a member of the Section I Wrestling Committee.

What is the best thing about your job?

Easy question: working with my students and student athletes. Everyone is so unique, and as a coach, I have to know what works and what doesn't work for each individual one. Some need a proverbial kick in the pants to motivate them while others need a pat on the back. Finding out what makes each one tick is a challenge but is absolutely necessary for them to achieve their goals. In wrestling, it is even more vital because team chemistry is not relevant; each individual athlete needs to work on their own skills so that when those are accomplished, the team will be successful. In wrestling, you are on the mat alone, and it is up to you, not a teammate, when the time comes to compete.

What is the most challenging thing about your job?

Over the years, it is the volume of paperwork that has greatly increased. It seems as if each year there is another form or another database that just adds more time to an already busy and hectic job.

Dealing with parents is also a challenge because they are often shocked at the time commitment required for interscholastic sports in high school. This also applies to the athletes once they get to the high school. There are two reasons for this, in my opinion. I went to a junior high school on Long Island. We practiced a solid two and a half hours every day, including holidays and Saturdays, and there were cuts and extreme competition to get playing time. But in the modified programs, we don't practice on holidays or on weekends, and playing time is somewhat given out to the players. Moving from the junior high to high school was a small step up the ladder, but moving from the modified to high school is a huge leap many are not prepared for. Another reason is that many kids have been given so many things (trophies for participating!) that they expect immediate gratification, and if they do not find success, they are not willing to put forth the long-term effort needed.

Who helped you the most in furthering your career and how?

My parents, for sure. My father was inducted into the National Wrestling and New York State Wrestling Hall of Fames, and so it was easy to admire what he had done. He was also my junior high lacrosse coach, my freshman soccer coach, and my high school wrestling coach. My mother came to every athletic event I participated in, and so I felt a great deal of support all the time. Now that he is retired, my father has become a volunteer assistant coach on my staff, which is quite awesome. Not only did I learn firsthand as an athlete what a great coach is, but with him on my staff, I often confer with him on ways to improve and how to handle certain situations. This is invaluable!

As a kid, did you think you would have this career when you grew up? Why or why not? What were your expectations?

I knew deep down that I enjoyed working with kids. I was the oldest grandchild on both sides of my family and had many younger cousins who I loved to teach things to. I also had a deep admiration for my father and some incredible teachers and coaches I met along the way and realized this was my calling. I love doing what I am doing and cannot imagine doing anything else in life.

What advice or tips can you give young people thinking of a career in your field?

To paraphrase Socrates, those who know they know nothing are truly the wisest. What I mean is be open to ideas, seek out those who have experience, be willing to admit your mistakes, and never stop growing. If you think you know everything, that is the surest sign you are blind to reality. Complacency is the sure path to burnout and failure. And always remember that success or failure is not measured in wins and losses but rather in not doing your best to reach each athlete who joins your team. They are not paid to be there. They are choosing to be there, so never take that for granted. Give them your best because, for you, there is another season and there will be another team but, for them, this is it.

Do you plan to stay in your career for a long time? If not, what do you think you will do after your career is over?

It has been twenty-one years since I began teaching and coaching, and I imagine I will be here until the day I retire.

What demands does your job put on your personal life? How do you deal with them?

There are many, many demands. I live thirty-five minutes away from where I work and teach. During wrestling season, which starts the first week in November and does not end until the very end of February, I am away every single Saturday. I leave my home at 6:15 AM each weekday, and if I don't have a dual meet that day, I will not get home until close to 7:00 PM. My wife is left to do much of the work while I am gone. It has also resulted in missed meals and missed quality family time together. But I am fortunate to have a

great assistant coach, so I can get home for [my own kids']
school concerts and plays. It was hardest when my children
were younger and is certainly something every coach needs
to take into account when [that person] makes the commitment to coach. I think it is the reason you rarely see the lifers
like my father and now like me.

WHO'S THE BOSS?

Coaches who are employed by schools are usually supervised by
the athletic director. A large school, such as a college, university,
or high school, might have its own athletic director. Other athletic
directors are employed by the school district and oversee coaches
and sports programs at all the schools, from elementary to high
school, in the district.

WHAT DOES AN ATHLETIC DIRECTOR DO ALL DAY?

- Coordinate and oversee athletic programs in schools

- Hire and manage staff

- Figure out budgets and raise money

- Make sure all programs meet school district and federal rules

- Negotiate broadcasting rights

- Negotiate business contracts

- Speak to the media and be the face of the sports program

- Write press releases

- Teach classes

- Attend sporting events and competitions

Anyone who is interested in becoming an athletic director should have a great love of both sports and people. You need to be able to hire the best staff and then manage them so they do the best job coaching their athletes. It's also important for an athletic director to have a good business sense and be able to balance budgets and raise money.

Accounting, business, social studies, math, and English courses will lay a great foundation for this career for high school students. A bachelor's degree in sports administration or physical education plus classes in business and management are required to get a job in this field. Once you have your degree, you can look for a position as a coach, physical education teacher, or assistant athletic director in order to gain experience and start your climb up the ladder.

Most athletic director positions pay well and offer benefits such as health insurance and paid vacations.

BIG LEAGUE *profile*

Name: Edward Benvenuto
Job: Teacher and coach, Clarkstown North High School, New City, New York

Why do you love sports?

I have participated in sports ever since I can remember. They have always served as an outlet for me. I have always enjoyed competing and pushing myself beyond what I thought was possible.

Why do you think it's important for young people to get involved in sports?

The rates of childhood obesity have been on the rise for far too long. The advances in modern technology make it so easy for a child to become lazy and out of shape. Sports can keep you in better health, help you feel better about yourself, and help you become a better manager of your time.

What was your professional journey? How did you get to where you are today?

I started to coach about twelve years ago as an assistant track coach up in Cornwall, New York. That started my love of coaching and spurred me on to my present positions at Clarkstown North, where I coach football and indoor and outdoor track and field.

What is a typical day like for you?

Since I teach and coach three sports, my regular school day ends around 2:00. Then I have about thirty minutes to myself, and then it's on to practice or competitions.

What education did you pursue to get a job in this career? What classes were particularly helpful?

My background in sports led me to pursue a career in coaching. My love and appreciation for sports is what keeps me going day after day.

What work or volunteer experiences helped you gain experience and contacts as you moved up in your career?

My timing was good, as there were open coaching positions when I started. Over the years I have coached, I have met many other coaches and observed their techniques and ideas to make myself a better coach.

What is the best thing about your job?
The best part is getting to know a bunch of student athletes who I normally don't get to see during the school day. Also, when an athlete makes a breakthrough in discipline, that can be the most rewarding thing as a coach. I always hope that the athletes I coach can eclipse what I was able to accomplish.

What is the most challenging thing about your job?
Trying everything in my bag of tricks, drills, and ideas to get athletes over their plateaus. Or athletes just not being able to perform physically. These are the most frustrating parts of my job.

Who helped you the most in furthering your career and how?
The list is too long. I thank everyone I have had the opportunity to speak to and learn from.

As a kid, did you think you would have this career when you grew up? Why or why not? What were your expectations?
I always saw myself playing sports for life, potentially professionally. However, professional athletics are reserved for a few.

What advice or tips can you give young people thinking of a career in your field?
Become a student of your sport. Learn as much as you can about your sport. Watch coaches and speak to other people who know more than you. Having knowledge in your area can only serve to help you.

Do you plan to stay in your career for a long time? If not, what do you think you will do after your career is over?

I do. I have no plans of stopping my career as a coach. If and when I do stop coaching, I would consider becoming a certified official and try to give back to a sport that I enjoyed for so long.

What demands does your job put on your personal life? How do you deal with them?
As with most things in life, there are trade-offs. I have been keeping a stringent schedule for quite some time now and have become accustomed to it. I live my life around my responsibilities.

INSTRUCTORS—A DIFFERENT KIND OF COACH

Not every athletic teacher is a coach at a school or for a sports team. Thousands of people earn their living teaching individuals about a specific sport on a one-to-one basis.

Certified Ski Instructors

Job Description: Teach everything from basic skills to more advanced techniques. Offer daily group classes or private lessons.

Education: Requires certification. Great for college students.

Job Locations: Approximately thirty-nine states have ski resorts. Most resorts are located in New England, the upper Midwest, California, Colorado, and Canada. Work is usually seasonal.

Lifeguards and Swimming Instructors

Job Description: Watch over swimmers and offer swimming and diving classes that can range from beginner classes to more advanced classes for all ages. Lifeguards have a big responsibility to keep people safe and enforce rules.

Education: Older high school students (age sixteen and up) and college students are ideal for this job. All lifeguards and instructors must be trained and certified. The basic lifeguard course lasts about a week and tests swimming skills as well as the ability to perform CPR and first aid. The American Red Cross offers certification for water safety instructors.

Job Locations: Public and private pools, beaches, camps, and health clubs anywhere in the country. Work is usually seasonal unless you are employed by a health club or other facility with an indoor pool or live in an area that is warm all year round.

SPOTLIGHT

Miranda Leek: Real-life Katniss Everdeen

Born in 1993 in Des Moines, Iowa, Miranda Leek found her athletic passion at age five, when her father, an amateur archer, taught her how to use a recurve bow. A recurve bow's tips curve away from the archer when the bow is strung. Though she learned archery on a recurve bow, Leek used a compound bow—modern bow that uses cables and pulleys to bend its limbs—until she switched back to recurve at age twelve. Though Leek works with professional coaches for team competitions, her dad remains her personal coach.

Leek was the sole women's archer at the 2010 Youth Olympic Games. And in the same year she started at Texas A&M University, she took silver in the US Nationals and, ranked seventh in the world, qualified for Team USA to attend the 2012 Olympics.

Leek's artistic passion is the piano and, thanks to the piano at her team training facility, she still plays. It helps her calm her nerves, she says.

Golf or Tennis Instructors

Job Description: Offer basic to advanced instruction to children and adults. Public and private golf courses often have a golf pro on staff to instruct golfers. Tennis and golf academies offer group and individual classes. These instructors may also be employed at resorts, camps, or parks.

Education: No certification required. Instructors should have at least a high school education.

Job Locations: Anywhere in the United States. Work can be seasonal if you are working at a golf course or a summer camp, but indoor instructors at an academy or school can work all year long.

Get Up, Stay Up!

Sometimes it's hard to stay motivated to exercise. Here are some tips:

1. Learn new exercises in a familiar setting.

2. Remember that you and your friends can do and like different activities. Experiment to discover what you like—and encourage your friends to do the same!

3. Reward yourself when you make progress!

4. Structure your workout so that a difficult activity is followed by an easier, more fun one.

5. Be consistent. When you don't meet your goals, decide how you can the next time and don't reward yourself until you do meet them.

Notes:

1. "Omar Vizquel Adjusts to Coaching after Retirment," *USA Today*, February 22, 2013, http://www.usatoday.com/story/sports/mlb/2013/02/22/omar-vizquel-adjusts-to-coaching-after-retirement/1940549/

2. "Modified Sports," Section 3 Athletics, accessed March 18, 2013, www.section3athletics.org/modified_sports.cfm

4

Finding Players: Sports Scouts

How is a team put together? Who finds the players who have the best chance of working well together as a team and—hopefully!—winning a championship? Teams could not exist without scouts to find players for them. This is an unusual and very rewarding career that might be right for you!

WHAT DOES A SCOUT DO?

Scouts usually work for the team's general manager and consult with the coaching staff and even with the team's owner. A sports scout looks for players who are a good fit for that particular team. To do this, scouts spend *a lot* of time attending sporting events. Scouts go to college and even high school games to scope out the players and see who looks like a good prospect to move up to the pros. (College teams also scout high school players to see if they would be a good asset for their school.) If you've ever attended a baseball game and seen someone sitting near home plate with a radar gun, measuring pitch speed, you likely saw a scout.

Scouts also get leads from players themselves. It is not unusual for a scout for a professional team to get emails or videos from players who want to play for that team. Scouts may also call players they're interested in. They find these players through word-of-mouth and also by checking a list published by the MLB that is updated every week. This list compiles all the players who were released from major league teams (mostly from those organizations' minor league teams). Scouts may then invite these players to a team tryout or even hold open tryouts for anyone who is interested.

A scout for a team may also observe players on other teams. This not only helps teams identify players they want to hire, but it also helps teams check out what their opponents are doing and devise strategies to beat them.

Name: Ned Rice
Job: Director of Major League Administration, Baltimore Orioles, Maryland

Why do you love sports?
I grew to love sports by playing them every day when I was growing up. Every day after school, I was outside playing baseball, basketball, football, or whatever else we came up

with. The more you play, the more interested you become in watching the best in the world play the same games you're playing with your friends. You could always watch all the local teams play on television, so I would watch as much as I could, which helped me learn more about each sport. Being at a sold-out sporting event when your favorite team wins and all the fans around you are going crazy cheering for your team is pretty special. Sports can give you the kinds of emotional ups and downs that are hard to understand or replace for people who don't play and follow sports.

DID YOU KNOW ...

The Major League Scouting Bureau (MLSB) is a professional scouting organization that the commissioner of Major League Baseball oversees. The MLSB employs about thirty-four full-time scouts and thirteen part-time scouts who report on players in the minor leagues. (You can find out how to contact the MLSB in chapter 11.)

The National Football League (NFL) and the National Basketball Association (NBA) have similar systems to scout players in their developmental leagues and teams in Europe.

Why do you think it's important for young people to get involved in sports?
To succeed in any sport takes practice and hard work, two important skills that help prepare you for the future. I think team sports can teach you even more. Learning to work with and care about others is so important, and few places teach that better than a team sport. This might not be quite as true at the younger ages when children are just trying to learn the game, but as you reach your teenage years and start playing on more advanced teams, you start to learn how important your teammates are to your own individual success.

What was your professional journey? How did you get to where you are today?

As my college graduation came closer, I realized how much I wanted to work in baseball. I asked everyone I knew if they had a connection and finally found a friend who had a friend who had interned in public relations (PR) with the Orioles. He gave me some advice, and I was able to get an interview for that internship. I was lucky in that I had graduated from college and had more free time, making me a more desirable candidate. I was lucky enough to be able to live at home so I could afford to intern, and I learned all about the inner workings of a baseball team. I always wanted to work in baseball operations, and my time in PR allowed me to network with the people in that department and eventually secure an internship in baseball operations. After a long time working for minimum wage, I was eventually hired and have been gaining experience and taking on more responsibility over the years.

What is a typical day like for you?

Every day is a little bit different. My main responsibility is to know all of the many rules that govern what we can and can't do in baseball operations and make sure that our decision makers know the most strategic way to operate within those rules. Depending on the time of year, I might be at spring training in Florida, watching a regular season game in Baltimore, or working in the office on contract negotiations for the upcoming season. No two days are alike, and they all involve baseball, which is what keeps the job so interesting.

What education did you pursue to get a job in this career? What classes were particularly helpful?

I didn't tailor my education to my career; I was a government major. My high school and college coursework certainly taught me how to think clearly, come up with logical solutions, and express my thoughts in meaningful and concise ways. But I learned just as much outside the classroom. I spent a lot of time in college in student government, and the on-the-job leadership training that provided is one of the most useful things I learned from college.

What work or volunteer experiences helped you gain experience and contacts as you moved up in your career?
I was pretty fortunate to land my first internship here, and then each of my steps up was the result of working hard and being well prepared, and then being in the right place at the right time.

What is the best thing about your job?
No matter how busy we are or how stressful a day can become, we're still all working in a game we love, which makes everything more interesting. When your team achieves success, as we did last year in surprising the baseball world and making the playoffs, it's an amazing feeling. Watching the city of Baltimore rally around the team was something I'll never forget.

What is the most challenging thing about your job?
We work hard to make the best decisions, but at the end of the day, our success is not determined by what we do but by how our players perform. We can acquire a player that we are excited about, and he can get hurt or perform at a level below what we were expecting. Conversely, sometimes a small move that we have low expectations for turns out to be tremendously valuable. We focus on improving our process every day, but there is so much uncertainty in baseball, and all of us—the players, coaches, and front office—are at the mercy of that to some extent.

> There's always a point where you get knocked down. But I draw on what I've learned on the track: if you work hard, things will work out.
>
> **Lolo Jones**
> TRACK-AND-FIELD ATHLETE

Who helped you the most in furthering your career and how?

So many people. The friend who found a friend of hers and got me an opportunity to interview for an internship. The PR employee who hired me for my first internship, and the leaders of baseball operations who hired me to join the department as an intern. I would never have had a chance to be where I am now without all those people looking out for me and giving me a chance. Once I was in that role, the two people who have mentored me the most are Andy MacPhail, our general manager who hired me full-time, and Matt Klentak, who was my direct boss and spent much of his time teaching me how to do all the things that he did. Andy gave me a meaningful role and responsibility, and was a tremendous leader by example. Watching his professionalism and leadership techniques in his role was a tremendous example to learn from. As for Matt, many people in competitive organizations are very careful to make sure nobody else knows how to do what they know how to do to ensure they remain valuable. Matt was the opposite; he thought he wasn't doing his job right unless he made sure somebody beneath him was learning the ins and outs of what he did, so that if he ever left, the organization would be able to stay strong. Matt left the Orioles for a job with the Angels after the 2011 season, and his mentorship allowed me to take on a lot of the tasks that Matt performed. Even though neither is with the organization any longer, I still call both of them with questions, and they are an invaluable source of insight and assistance.

> **FAST FACT**
>
> Not all sports are featured in the Olympics. A committee decides if a sport should be added or taken away. For example, baseball was an Olympic sport between 1992 and 2008 but was not included in the 2012 Olympics.

As a kid, did you think you would have this career when you grew up? Why or why not? What were your expectations?

Not really, oddly enough. I always loved sports and loved baseball but didn't really consider a career in the field until I was approaching my college graduation.

What advice or tips can you give young people thinking of a career in your field?

It's such a competitive field. So many unbelievably qualified people are willing to work for free for a chance at a job. With so many applicants, you have to try to stand out and have things on your résumé that other people don't have. If you want to be an analyst, make sure you have top-notch database skills or, better yet, learn how to be a computer programmer. If you want to scout, get out to games, meet scouts, ask them questions, learn from them, and write your own reports. People skills are incredibly important. We spend so much time together at the office that we might shy away from hiring a qualified applicant who doesn't fit into the office culture smoothly. Lastly, have a backup plan. No matter how prepared you are, you need to get a little bit lucky. You might find yourself approaching thirty and having just worked at different internships for the last five years and still without a job. At some point, you might need to pull the plug and make a living in a different field.

Do you plan to stay in your career for a long time? If not, what do you think you will do after your career is over?

I think so. It's such a time-intensive job, and so many people who stay in this field for their careers end up

> You are never really playing an opponent. You are playing yourself, your own highest standards, and when you reach your limits, that is real joy.
>
> **Arthur Ashe**
>
> TENNIS PLAYER

moving several times throughout their career, so it's a difficult job for raising a family. I'm not married and don't have kids, so it's a dream job for me. I'd like to be able to work in this field my whole career, but it's always important to balance work and personal lives, so that's something I'll have to be constantly reevaluating throughout my career.

What demands does your job put on your personal life? How do you deal with them?
It's certainly tricky. We work long hours, and even though we have no games in the off-season, we are even busier preparing for the following season. I don't have to travel as much as some of our employees do, but it can still be difficult fitting in time for all the other things you want to do. You can usually sneak in a day or two off every now and then if you need, but it's hard to ever go away for a week or two, which makes any kind of international travel or real vacation nearly impossible. That's certainly the downside of the job, but you just try to balance everything as best you can given the circumstances.

What is your salary or compensation?
Most people have to take unpaid or minimum-wage internships for several seasons before they get hired, and once they get hired, the entry-level salaries are quite low. It's certainly not the right industry to get into if you're trying to get rich. Even as you start to make a little bit more money, it's still awfully low when you break it down into an hourly rate. Some of these internships are simply not affordable unless you can secure very low-cost housing. It's a great thrill to work in baseball, but the people who work here aren't drawn to the industry for the pay—we're drawn to the excitement of working for a team and working together for the common goal of trying to win a World Series.

SCOUT SLANG[1]

Baseball scouts have their own slang. Here are a few examples:

Barney Rubble. Player who is short and stocky, like the character in the *Flintstones* cartoon

Base Clogger. Slow runner

Bat Boy. Player who is physically small

Burner. Fast base runner

DNF. Draft and follow (player who should be signed to a contract)

KP. Can't play

NP. Non-prospect

Plowhorse. Player who keeps on trying after most people would have given up

Soft Tosser. Pitcher who throws off-speed pitches

SPOTLIGHT

Billy Beane:
King of the Numbers Game

Baseball scouts loved Billy Beane when he was a high school baseball star. In 1980, after he finished high school, the San Diego resident signed with the New York Mets. However, Beane had trouble adjusting to the demands of professional baseball and didn't rise to the major leagues as fast as he and everyone else expected. Instead, he played for a number of minor league teams, occasionally moving up to play with the Mets for a few games at a time. Meanwhile, Beane saw other players with less physical talent do better because they had more determination and focus than he did.

The Mets traded Beane to the Minnesota Twins in 1985, and he continued to bounce back and forth between the majors and the minors. After he was traded to the Detroit Tigers and then the Oakland Athletics, Beane was tired of the life of a minor league player. He asked Oakland's general manager, Sandy Alderson, if he could have a job as a baseball scout instead. In 1993, he was promoted to assistant general manager and took on even more scouting responsibilities.

Alderson taught Beane about a system called sabermetrics, which uses statistics to measure a baseball player's performance. Using this system, Beane zeroed in on high school and minor league players who had a high on-base percentage (often known as on-base average or OBA) but had been overlooked by other teams. This approach fit in well with Oakland's budget, as they were trying to spend less money on player salaries and still field a competitive team. Beane succeeded Alderson as general manager in 1997. Under his leadership and statistical savvy, the Athletics reached the playoffs several times. In 2002, they became the first American League team to win twenty consecutive games.

Beane's approach was so controversial and unusual that noted sports author Michael Lewis wrote a book about him. *Moneyball* was published in 2003 and became a popular movie starring Brad Pitt as Beane in 2011. Beane led his team using numbers to craft a lean, mean machine that could win ball games. What a great example of someone who succeeded behind the scenes in sports!

How Do I Get There?

If you're interested in becoming a scout, you should spend as much time as possible studying players on your school or local teams.

Working with coaches will help you figure out what qualities are good and what makes a player stand out. It's also good to practice taking notes and keeping records. You will become a master of statistics if you're interested in this job.

A NEW EVENT FOR NEW ATHLETES

Only two games old, the 2010 and 2012 events, the Youth Olympic Games are an elite sporting event for athletes ages fifteen to eighteen. They include the Culture and Education Program based around five themes: Olympism, Social Responsibility, Skills Development, Expression, and Well-being and Healthy Lifestyles.

The summer games features twenty-eight sports, the winter games seven, and they support some sports different from those in the adult Olympic Games, such as three-on-three basketball and mixed-gender events.

Programs for young reporters, ambassadors, and athlete role models ensure that sports lovers who aren't athletes can also participate in the games.

General high school courses can prepare you for a career as a scout. Speech and English courses are a great way to improve communication and writing skills, while math and computer classes will help you with the numbers work you'll need to do. It's also great to learn a foreign language (particularly Spanish) to make it easier to communicate with the many foreign players who come to the United States to play. Of course, it goes without saying that physical education classes are a must and playing on or volunteering on a school team is a big help too.

There are no colleges that offer classes in scouting, but some teams do run scout schools to train employees. (The Major League Scouting Bureau runs one of these schools. See chapter 11.) Other scouts sort of fall into the career by accident, as you'll see in the interview below.

A good sports scout is also detail-oriented, very organized, good at communicating, and able to see what's best for the team or organization. A thorough knowledge of the rules of the sport you're interested in is also essential.

Bringing Home the Bacon

There are about one thousand sports scouts working in the United States. The job is not that well paying. Many scouts for minor league or independent teams are only compensated for expenses or receive a small stipend. For this reason, most scouts at this level also work other jobs. Of course, you do get to go to lots of games and sporting events for free.

Name: Kevin Tuve
Job: Scout, Rockland Boulders baseball team, Pomona, New York

Why do you love sports?

I have loved sports, particularly baseball, hockey, and basketball, most of my life. I love the lessons learned, how hard work can pay off, and the people you meet. I have met such wonderful people being involved in sports.

Why do you think it's important for young people to get involved in sports?

It's important for young kids to get involved in sports for a few reasons: the discipline you learn is priceless, and the people you meet can build bonds and friendships that can last a lifetime. Young people can see that in life there are going to be ups and downs on the way to your goals.

What was your professional journey? How did you get to where you are today?

I began coaching in 1998 at Paramus Catholic High School in New Jersey. It began my coaching career in girls basketball, and that lasted through 2006. I went from being a freshman coach to later being named Bergen County Women's Coach of the Year and *Herald News* Coach of the Year in 2006. I then began my baseball journey in 2010 with the Pittsfield Colonials of the Can-Am League. I stayed with Pittsfield for both the 2010 and 2011 seasons, and then the team folded. I became an associate scout with the Seattle Mariners from March 2012 through July. It was in July that the Boulders brought me on board to work in the player development department.

What is a typical day like for you?

It depends. During the school year, I am teaching at Lodi High School in New Jersey. I teach history to grades nine and eleven. So it's not until after school that I get to return calls and emails for baseball. In the summer, I am all baseball from morning until after the games at night. I enjoy the workload, but it can be challenging to do everything in the same day.

What education did you pursue to get a job in this career? What classes were particularly helpful?

I went to school to teach history. Sports was just a hobby and big part of who I am. I never was a sports management major in college, so I never took any sports classes.

What work or volunteer experiences helped you gain experience and contacts as you moved up in your career?

The contacts started when I began scouting in 2010. It's not the money that drives me. It's the type of work that gives me a sense of accomplishment. When I came to Pittsfield in 2010, I saw how contacts have to be made all along the way.

What is the best thing about your job?

The best thing about my job is seeing a player get signed, especially players who you have kept your eye on for a long period of time. I like to receive calls, emails, or tips on players. I just never know who will be contacting me looking for a position anywhere around the nation.

What is the most challenging thing about your job?

The most difficult thing would be determining who to call back and who to pass on. You need to do research to see which players are leads and which are not worth all the effort. I follow every lead I can and give everyone an equal opportunity to state their experience, hunger, or simply their will to play baseball. Also, one tough aspect about independent baseball is keeping your emotions out of your work. In other words, don't think every player can do this.

> The only disability in life is a bad attitude.
>
> **Scott Hamilton**
>
> FIGURE SKATER

Who helped you the most in furthering your career and how?

I would say I have received very valuable help along the way from: Robert Seaman (owner of the Pittsfield Colonials); Brian Daubach (Pittsfield Colonials); Jamie Keefe (manager of the Pittsfield Colonials and now the Rockland Boulders); John Burns (my associate); my father, Al Tuve; and Shawn Reilly and Ken Lehner, who are the

Rockland Boulders' owners. All of these gentlemen have shown me parts of this business that I would never would have seen before.

Robert Seaman gave me my first opportunity in June of 2010. He, along with Brian and Jamie, showed me that you need to be tough and particular when it comes to judging talent. They also showed me that the connections you make need to be utilized and followed when referencing a player. Shawn and Ken gave me a wonderful opportunity in player development. They understand how being organized and efficient gets the best results in whatever

you have to do. I like to work really hard for them since they did something special by bringing baseball to this area in 2010. John is my sounding board. I contact him five to six times each day! We check on leads, players, agents, and whatever are that day's topics. I can't even begin to describe the amount of thought John puts into this. My dad just keeps me sharp when it comes to some decisions I may make in baseball. [Since he's] a retired teacher, it helps to have him to bounce ideas off of as well.

As a kid, did you think you would have this career when you grew up? Why or why not? What were your expectations?

No, I never thought I would be scouting, but I always wanted to get involved in sports. I would love to do player development for a Major League team someday. I just never had a connection to get into the game. I had unrealistic expectations like any other young kid growing up a fan.

What advice or tips can you give young people thinking of a career in your field?

Don't expect to fall into a position. Volunteer as much as you are able to. Work so hard that you impress yourself and others. Don't ever give up, and respect others as well as this game of baseball.

Do you plan to stay in your career for a long time? If not, what do you think you will do after your career is over?

I would love to stay in this game somehow for as long as possible. I plan to try and do that and hope for the best after that. I just love the opportunity given to me for now.

What demands does your job put on your personal life? How do you deal with them?

There are crazy hours and no days off. Baseball can cramp your time sometimes, but you learn to live with it. My girlfriend is patient and knows that certain times call for certain calls to be made. The key is unlimited minutes for my cell phone. I have to find the right times to make calls or do emails. Some days are busier than others. I try to manage the best I can, but it is up to me to make it work.

> Focus, discipline, hard work, goal setting, and, of course, the thrill of finally achieving your goals. These are all lessons in life.
>
> **Kristi Yamaguchi**
> FIGURE SKATER
>
>

What is your salary or compensation?

I receive a stipend for what I do.

Why do you love being a scout for an independent baseball team?

It's more interesting than working for a Major League team. You can bring in people from all over the world. With minor league teams affiliated to majors, you're given a list of players to scout, so you don't have as much freedom.

Notes:

1. Lee Lowenfish, "A Century's Worth of Stories," *Memories and Dreams: Opening Day 2013*, 35, no. 2 (2013), 14–17.

5

I Call a Penalty:
Referees and Other Officials

Long ago, there were no rules and pretty much anything was fair when it came to sports. However, as athletics became more organized, rules and regulations were drawn up, and officials were put in place to make sure these rules were followed. Today, every sport has its own set of rules—usually enough to fill a thick book! And every sport has referees, umpires, and other officials to make sure everyone plays fairly.

FAST FACT

Boxing, rugby, and soccer were the first sports to have trained officials.

DIFFERENT SPORTS, DIFFERENT RULES

Every sport has its own rules and regulations. To make things even more complicated, the same sport played on different levels has its own distinct rules. For example, in basketball, the team that has the ball usually has a limited time to shoot the ball. In professional basketball, the shot clock is twenty-four seconds. But guess what? In men's college basketball, the shot clock is thirty-five seconds, and women's college basketball uses a thirty-second shot clock. Most high school basketball games do not use a shot clock at all.

If there is more than one official monitoring a game, each referee takes a different position on the field. For example, in baseball, there is a home plate umpire as well as three other umpires stationed near the bases. Basketball and football referees are stationed around the court or field, and each has a specific area to observe. In hockey, three referees or umpires skate up and down the ice, watching the players. In addition, a penalty timekeeper keeps track of penalty times served, while two goal judges watch shots on the goals to make sure if a goal has been scored or not.

THE RULING ON THE FIELD IS . . .

Just as there are different rules for different sports, there are different numbers of officials on the field at any given time. Here's a look at some of the official numbers for a variety of sports, per game.

MLB: 4 umpires

Little League baseball: 1 umpire

NBA: 3 referees

College and high school basketball: 2–3 referees

Grade school basketball: 2 referees

NFL: 4–7 referees

NHL: 3 officials on the ice and 3 off the ice

Stop the Game!

Whenever an official sees someone breaking the rules, he or

she blows a whistle. Play usually stops until the problem is sorted out and a penalty is given. Penalties can be given if a player has unnecessary contact with another player or is in the wrong position, to list just two examples. Officials also decide such issues as whether a ball is fair or foul and whether a goal was actually scored. A track or swimming official makes sure that all athletes start at the same time and no one gets a head start.

Referees, umpires, and other officials consult rule books, but most of the time, all the information you need is in your head. In some sports, plays can be reviewed using instant-replay cameras, which allow officials to make sure the calls they make are correct. However, in most sports, the referees call 'em as they see 'em, and whatever decision made is the last word.

SPOTLIGHT

Edward G. Hochuli: Using His Mind On and Off the Field

If you're watching a professional football game and you see a referee wearing the number 85 on his uniform, you're watching one of the most famous and popular refs in the sport: Edward G. Hochuli. He has been an NFL official since the 1990 season and officiated in two Super Bowls.

Hochuli was born on December 25, 1950, in Milwaukee, Wisconsin. He played football growing up and was a linebacker on the University of Texas at El Paso (UTEP) team between 1969 and 1972. After earning a law degree from the University of Arizona in 1976, he became a partner in the law firm of Jones, Skelton & Hochuli in 1983.

Along with working hard at his law career, Hochuli stayed active in football. When he was a postsecondary student, one of his high school coaches suggested he officiate as a way to earn extra money. Hochuli took the coach's advice and began officiating at Pop Warner football games. He also worked as a Little League baseball umpire between 1970 and 1973. Hochuli then moved on to officiate many high school football games in the Tucson area. He also spent many years as a college official in the Big Sky and Pacific-10 (Pac-10) Conferences.

Hochuli applied to work in the NFL in 1989 and was invited to join in 1990. His first jobs were as a field judge and a back judge. Hochuli learned from experience and from other referees he worked with. In 1992, he was promoted to referee. Asked by *USA Today* in 2007 to compare being a lawyer with being a referee, Hochuli once said, "A trial is nothing, pressure-wise, compared to the NFL."

Hochuli takes football very seriously, explaining the penalties he calls, often in great detail. He has become so popular and well-known that he has been mentioned in talk-show host's David Letterman's Top Ten List and his likeness appears in the Madden NFL series of video games for the Xbox 360. Hochuli also appeared on the cover of the October 8, 2012, issue of *Sports Illustrated*.

Getting Ready

How can you prepare for a career in officiating? Just like being on the playing field, it's best to start early and seize any opportunity you can. Here are some ideas:

In high school, learn as much as you can about the sport you are interested in. Get a rule book and memorize it! Volunteer to be a timekeeper at your school's basketball games or officiate at a Little League game or games at a local program. Volunteering is a great way to gain experience and meet people who share your love of sports and may be able to give you a hand in furthering your career.

As far as classes, English classes such as speech, debate, and theater will help you build your self-confidence and speak clearly. Sociology and psychology courses will help you understand people and be able to understand and get along with them. Finally, most people who hope to be a referee need to be physically active. Just look at how much running a basketball or hockey referee does. And obviously, a hockey umpire has to be an excellent ice skater. So do your best in gym class and work out, especially by running, biking, or doing other cardio. After all, you can't call a penalty if you didn't see the action because you were huffing and puffing on the sidelines.

Being an official doesn't require a four-year college degree, and there are no specific postsecondary programs that provide a degree in this field. However, most sports officials do go to college. As in high school, classes in communications and sociology are a good bet, along with participation in athletic activities.

There are special training schools that offer classes in officiating. For example, the International Association of Approved Basketball Officials has several schools that run summer programs. Officials can also train for Major League Baseball umpire positions at the Jim Evans Academy of Professional Umpiring and the Harry Wendelstedt Umpire School. These training programs also provide certification for umpires and referees, which is necessary for anyone hoping to work as an official. Programs are taught by professional officials and feature a review of the rules as well as game situations to teach umpires and referees how to act on the field.

You'll find more information about all these organizations in chapter 11.

There is one more thing to keep in mind if you're interested in a career as an official, and this is nothing you can learn in the classroom: a referee or umpire has to be able to stay cool under pressure. A player, coach, or manager might not like the call you made and argue with you. Spectators in the stands aren't shy about heaping abuse on referees who made what they believe to be a bad call. It's important that officials keep their cool and don't react negatively to being yelled at or worse. It's also important for officials to have the strength of character to make unpopular decisions and stand by them calmly and firmly. A hotheaded ref with a bad temper will not go far in this career.

Moving On Up

Sports officials work in professional and semi-professional sports leagues, schools, youth leagues, and sports organizations. As with just about any career, no one starts at the top. The best way to get started is to volunteer or work part time on the local level. You'll also want to look into certification.

Many officials start working with youth leagues and then move up to officiating amateur adult competitions. The next step would be college games, professional minor league games and, for a select few, a position in the major leagues.

Just like most athletes aspire to the big leagues but never get there, becoming a big league umpire or referee in any sport is very difficult. For baseball umpires, for example, the minor league is a testing and training ground. An umpire spends an average of six to eight years working at the minor league level before he is even considered for a major league umpiring job. In other sports, such as football, officials must have ten years of experience including time at the college level before they can work in the big leagues. Even if you are ready for the big leagues, there might not be a spot for you there. Umpires in the major leagues rarely leave the job and work until retirement. During one ten-year period, MLB's American League hired only three new umpires. It's up to expansion teams and new leagues to create more job opportunities.

Name: Ann Tembruell
Job: Official, YMCA swim meets, Escanaba, Michigan

Why do you love sports?
I was never involved in any sports when I was growing up unless it was a fun game in the neighborhood. I liked to watch them but wasn't a participant. It has only been since I've had kids who are involved that I am involved.

Why do you think it's important for young people to get involved in sports?
What we absolutely love about swimming is that it is more of a mental battle with yourself, rather than a competition with others. It's also team oriented, as the scoring of points for your placement in a race adds to the point total for the team.

What is a typical day like for you?

A typical day at swim meet for an official starts off with getting your assignment. Depending on the number of officials working that meet, you may be assigned a broad area or a smaller area. The last meet that I was an official at this season I was one of only two! That hasn't been typical. I had to cover not only starts and finishes but the length of half the pool. At that meet, I also was the person who pressed the starter signal, so duties can be varied. Most often at the meets I've worked, I've been a turn judge. I stand at the end of the pool that does not have the starting blocks and watch that all turns at the twenty-five-yard end are complete and regulation. Each of the four competitive strokes has its particular correct way to make the turn. But the main purpose of a swim official is to inform swimmers of improper technique. It's not to penalize the swimmers or make them feel bad but to teach better skills.

FAST FACT

The Paralympic Games began as an event for injured soldiers and were held in the United Kingdom at the same time as the 1948 Olympics were held in London.

What education did you pursue to get a job in this career?

The process is fairly easy. You take a daylong class by a certified trainer. I am lucky that at our Y we have one of the country's leading trainers as a member. She trains all over the Midwest plus often officiates at the YMCA Spring Nationals competition.

Once you complete the course, you take an online exam. If you pass, you get your certification.

I am a Level 1 official, which basically means I need at least one Level 2 official to be my boss at a swim meet. You can become a Level 2 official only after being a Level 1 for a certain amount of time. I am required to work a total of twelve meets within a three-year time period to qualify for recertification.

What work or volunteer experiences helped you gain experience and contacts as you moved up in your career?

At the beginning of each swim season, volunteers are sought to be certified as YMCA officials. I had thought it sounded interesting when my older daughter, Claire, first started on the team. Since she needed a lot of help getting to her events and keeping track of things, I waited until she was older and more experienced. It wasn't until my younger daughter, Lydia, had been on the team a couple years that I decided to be certified.

I did lots of other jobs at the swim meets before trying the official route. It's just another experience that helps me better understand the sport.

TOP TEN SPORTS MASCOTS IN 2013[1]

The Davie Brown Index measured the appeal and effectiveness of pro sports mascots. Here are some of the mascots who do the most good for their teams:

1. The Phillie Phanatic (Philadelphia Phillies)

2. The San Diego Chicken (formerly with the San Diego Padres, so popular that the mascot now freelances)

3. The Racing Sausages (Milwaukee Brewers)

4. Mr. Met (New York Mets)

5. The Gorilla (Phoenix Suns)

6. The Racing Presidents (Washington Nationals)

7. Benny the Bull (Chicago Bulls)

8. Wally the Green Monster (Boston Red Sox)

9. Rocky (Denver Nuggets)

10. Billy the Marlin (Florida Marlins)

What's the best thing about your job?

The best thing is that I have a prime spot to watch my kids swim! I can always see them clearly.

What's the most challenging thing about your job?

The most challenging is keeping track of the different incorrect nuances in strokes and turns. It really depends on where you are looking and when. If you are covering many areas, it is very hard to ensure legal races, especially as the swimmers get faster and closer together in abilities. It's always a relief to have another judge as a backup set of eyes.

Who helped you the most in furthering your career and how?

I've learned a lot from the more experienced officials. They explain lots of the ins and outs of technique—that knowledge only comes with practice being an official.

As a kid, did you think you would have this career when you grew up? Why or why not? What were your expectations?

No, never thought I'd be doing it.

WHAT ABOUT WOMEN?

For most of sports' history, all officials were men. That began to change with the creation of women's professional leagues in basketball and soccer. History was made in 1997 when two women, Dee Kantner and Violet Palmer, became the first female referees to officiate NBA games. However, the truth remains that most officials are men.

What advice or tips can you give young people thinking of a career in your field?
Give it a try!

Do you plan to stay in your career for a long time? If not, what do you think you will do after your career is over?
I do plan on renewing my certificate this fall. I don't plan on moving up to the Level 2 certification at this time.

What demands does your job put on your personal life? How do you deal with them?
The biggest problem has been that my children are always worried I will disqualify them. The officials working the meets try hard to not oversee our own kids for just that reason. Sometimes it isn't possible, and we have to remain impartial no matter what. I tell my kids that I will treat them just like any other swimmer while they are in the pool.

The Paycheck

Most officiating jobs do not pay very well. Officials at top colleges or in major league sports can make much more, and officials who work big events such as the Super Bowl or the World Series get bonuses. Officials also get additional money to cover travel costs, hotel bills, and food expenses while on the road. Officials at school and amateur levels are paid by the game, although many officials are volunteers.

Like becoming a professional athlete, becoming a top-level official is a big dream that few people achieve. However, this can be a great career if you enjoy sports and want to be part of the action. It's also a good part-time career or a way to make extra money and still be part of the sports world.

Notes:

1. Sammy Said, "10 Most Popular Sports Mascots in America," The Richest, April 20, 2011, http://www.therichest.org/sports/mascots-in-america/ and "America's Favorite Sports Mascots," *Forbes*, accessed June 20, 2013, http://www.forbes.com/pictures/eddf45glmh/americas-favorite-sports-mascots/.

6

Tell Me Where It Hurts: Physical Therapists, Doctors, and Other People in Sports Medicine

Athletes cannot perform to the best of their abilities if they are not healthy and strong. Even the most powerful and physically fit athlete is going to suffer an injury at one time or another. Sports physicians and trainers are the ones who run to the rescue and get the athlete back into fighting shape again.

THE HISTORY OF SPORTS MEDICINE

Sports medicine has been around almost as long as sports itself. Hundreds of years ago, scientists and philosophers like Leonardo da Vinci and Aristotle studied the human body, how it moved and how different body systems worked together. Later, during the nineteenth century, a Frenchman named Étienne-Jules Marey did extensive work to study things like the amount of force exerted by a foot hitting the floor. He also took photos showing the different ways body parts moved as an athlete ran. Marey is considered by many to be the father of sports medicine.

It's amazing to think about it, but even a simple movement such as taking a step or throwing a ball requires an enormous amount of coordination among muscles, tendons, nerves, eyes, and other parts of the body. It's easy for things to go wrong, especially if part of the body is overused. Think of a baseball pitcher who wears out his elbow or his shoulder from all that throwing or a runner who injures her leg because she lands wrong on her foot. All of these motions have been studied by scientists to allow doctors to find the best way to prevent and treat injuries.

Name: Elizabeth Bennett
Age: 21
Job (when not studying!): Swimmer, Sacred Heart University, Connecticut
Dream Job: Physical therapist

What sports have you participated in and when?
Growing up, I played various sports and was part of several activities. I joined my local swim team when I was ten but did

not start becoming competitive until I was about twelve. It soon became my passion. I trained with a local club team and traveled in and out of state competitions during high school. In high school I also joined the cross-country and track teams. I feel that this transition was easy for me because swimming and running are sports that are most used for cross-training.

What are you doing now in terms of education/sports participation?
I am a member of my university's NCAA Division I swimming team. I was attracted to Sacred Heart because of academic and athletic purposes. When I was searching for colleges, I knew I wanted to swim at the Division I level, and I was interested in a profession in physical therapy. Sacred Heart offers an exercise science degree, which will aid in grad school. Sacred Heart also has a doctorate of physical therapy program, which I have been accepted into.

How did you get started in sports?
I was pretty active when I was younger, but I only got into sports when I was about ten years old. I remember watching the 2000 Summer Olympic Games and being fascinated with the swimming events. Hearing the swimmers' stories and watching them compete was so amazing, and it got me interested in the sport. I took swim lessons when I was about five, so I knew how to swim. I just didn't join a team once I graduated from all of the swim levels. It's incredible to me that I joined a swim club on a whim, and the sport became such as huge factor in my life.

What do you like best about sports?
The best thing I've been given from sports is the passion that

> Those who do not find time for exercise will have to find time for illness.
>
> **Edward Stanley**
> EARL OF DERBY
>
>

I feel whenever I participate in them. I feel this way about swimming, and I remember feeling this way when I was in cross-country and track in high school. Of course, the sports I joined are more individualized, but I think that is what makes them so worthwhile. I know that I am putting the effort into my races and technique, so when I get the results I want, it is so much more rewarding. I thrive on the adrenaline and competition. I have a competitive nature, which makes me focused. Finally, sports give me a purpose. As a student athlete, swimming and school are the two main things I am working toward in college. Swimming has given me the opportunity to have an education, to meet a wonderful group of friends, and to learn skills, such as time management, that I can use in life.

Do you plan to stay in sports for a long time?
I feel that swimming and running will always be a part of my life. It's hard to invest much of your life in something and just completely give it up when your athletic career is over. Of course, after I graduate college, I will focus more on my studies in grad school, but I can see myself getting back in the water and working out or running outside once in a while.

What are your career goals and dreams?
My career goals and dreams include certain goal times that I want to reach before I graduate. Most of my goals relate to how I perform at our conference championship meet at the end of the season, but there are other goals that I would like to accomplish that are not related to swimming. I want to come to practice with a positive attitude and contribute my positive attitude to the team. We are a small group of individuals, but whenever we have a tough workout or a challenging meet, we always come together and try to push through the obstacles. As a rising senior, I hope to be a role model for my younger teammates, especially the incoming freshmen. Most of all, I want to give 110 percent this upcoming year. Sadly,

this will be my last year of competitive swimming, but that makes me more determined than ever to make the most of it this upcoming season.

What advice or tips can you give young people thinking of a career in sports?

The best advice I could give someone who is considering a sports-related career is to love what you do. As an exercise science major, I know that some of the classes and workload seem unbearable, but I need to get through them in order to reach my goal of being a physical therapist. Someone once told me, "Don't live to work; work to live." That is something that keeps me going when I get discouraged in school. People interested in a sports-related career must be sure that this is what they truly want to do. If their heart is in it, then they will surely benefit from what they are studying and will be happy with their career in the future.

THE DOCTOR IS IN

The term *sports medicine* covers a number of different careers, including:

- Sports physicians
- Orthopedists (doctors who specialize in bones and muscles)
- Sports psychologists
- Athletic trainers
- Physical therapists

JUST WHAT THE DOCTOR ORDERED

Sports physicians treat injuries and illnesses in athletes, both professional and amateur. Some physicians work for teams and only care for the athletes on that team. Similarly, sports physicians who work for universities handle the medical needs of the student athletes at that school. Other sports physicians have independent practices and see any athlete who has an injury. These doctors or regular physicians might also visit local schools to care for athletes, perform physicals, and do other medical checkups.

Orthopedists and orthopedic surgeons are especially necessary in the sports medicine field, treating common athletic ills such as sprains, fractures, injured joints, and muscle damage. These doctors also create rehabilitation programs and work closely with athletic trainers and physical therapists.

Sports physicians often attend team practices and games. Being present allows you to monitor athletes who may need help, such as an athlete who gets overheated on a hot day or an athlete who is injured. Sports physicians are also able to perform first aid and determine if more serious medical help is needed. Many doctors enjoy being present at games and call this one of the best things about the job. One sports physician said that he loves "covering sports events and feeling a part of the action on the sidelines, in the locker room, or in the heat of the battle."[1]

> Surpassing my achievements feels incredible; I want to replicate that again and again.
>
> **Katherine Reutter**
>
> SPEED SKATER

You need a medical degree to become a sports physician or orthopedist. Anyone who is interested in a medical career should take as many health and science courses as possible in high school. Courses like biology and chemistry are especially important. Future sports physicians should then go on to a premed program at a college or university and then move on to medical school. After years of school, internships, and medical residencies, doctors generally have to take written and oral exams in order to get a license to practice medicine. From there, the doctor can go on to join the staff of a team, school, or hospital, or go into private practice.

Other than school, potential physicians should look for volunteer and on-the-job experience while still in school. Doctors in the field suggest working with athletic trainers at your school, volunteering or working at a local hospital or rehab center, and working or volunteering at a doctor's office.

Becoming a sports physician is a long, hard road, but the benefits can be tremendous. Along with helping people feel better and perform at their best, doctors are also well paid (although they usually have a lot of student loans to pay off!).

Keep Moving While Sitting!

Even if you can't run or jump, you can still have fun!

Warm-Up: Throw a ball back and forth with a friend. Lift weights.

Wheelchair Dance: Learn coordinated dance steps that involve moving forward, backward, and from side to side. Do dances that focus on a lot of upper body movements.

Race: Challenge your friends to an obstacle course you wheel through, or see how many basketballs you can get through a hoop in a minute.

Parachute: Gather your friends in a circle and hold a big piece of fabric. Move the parachute up and down, coordinating the movement.

Bubbles: While one person blows bubbles, the others race around tracking and popping them!

Cool Down: Stretch your arms. Listen to some music while you turn your head this way and that and wiggle your fingers.

MIND OVER MATTER

Sometimes, the way athletes think is just as important as how they feel physically. Sports psychologists are specially trained doctors who work with athletes to improve their mental and physical health and their athletic performance. They use goal setting, imagery, focusing strategies, relaxation techniques, and mental preparation to help athletes both on and off the field. They may work with individual athletes or entire teams.

Sports psychologists can be divided into three groups:

Clinical sports psychologists work with individuals who are experiencing emotional problems connected to their sport. For example, suppose an athlete has a fear of failure or believes he or she is not able to complete a task. The clinical psychologist works with that athlete to create coping strategies and ways to overcome the problem.

Educational sports psychologists teach students in a classroom setting and may also assist coaches on the field, teaching mental skills to help athletes perform.

Research sports psychologists conduct studies to come up with scientific facts and figures that help clinical and educational psychologists do their work. These studies are usually done in a laboratory or other testing facility.

Like the course of study for a sports physician, the educational requirements for a sports psychologist are strict. Students should take a wide variety of courses in high school, particularly English, math, science, psychology, and foreign languages. Of course, taking part in sports will give you insight into how athletes' minds work and what problems they might have. Students then need to complete college and get an advanced degree, a doctorate, to become a psychologist. You may opt for a

> **FAST FACT**
>
> Eating the right food is essential for an athlete. An athlete's diet depends on the sport. For sports that require a lot of energy, an athlete might consume six thousand calories a day—about three times the calories needed by the average adult.

PhD, which qualifies you for teaching, research, and counseling positions, or a PsyD, or Doctor of Psychology, degree. This degree is generally required for doctors who want to do clinical research. There are no programs that specifically train sports psychologists, so a general PhD or PsyD is your best bet.

Name: Garret Kramer
Job: Founder and managing partner, Inner Sports

Why do you love sports?
I really don't know. It was part of my life and how I grew up, so I guess it's just habit.

Why do you think it's important for young people to get involved in sports?
In principle, sports on their own can't teach lessons. The value is in you, so don't look for something outside of yourself (like sports) to provide answers. Being active has physical benefits, of course. But don't be a narrow-minded athlete. Sports are great but, contrary to what most people think is true, they are not a vehicle to directly teach leadership, discipline, or teamwork.

What is a typical day like for you?
When I started Inner Sports, most of my day was spent doing counseling sessions and teaching. Over the last couple years, I've been doing more writing and speaking engagements. However, I still work with players, coaches, parents, and even business leaders.

What education did you pursue to get a job in this career?

I have no degrees in this field. It was something I came up with through my own study and experiences.

What work or volunteer experiences helped you gain experience and contacts as you moved up in your career?

I grew up around ice sports. My dad managed a skating rink and was a hockey coach. I played hockey and coached, and was also a competitive amateur golfer. Then I went to Hamilton College in New York State, where I played hockey and majored in history. After I graduated, I worked in the construction business, but I kept coaching a high school hockey team on the side. So I became interested in athletes' mental ability—what was happening in their heads? When I was having trouble with my own game, I looked for help, but the resources I found only gave short-term help. They had no staying power with me or with the athletes I coached. I figured that I had to be missing something about the mental side of sports. I realized that using mental strategies to help someone who is struggling is like finding fool's gold. I decided that when I was struggling, I would not try to change. I would just keep living and see what happened. Guess what? It worked! Doing nothing to fix my mental state led to feeling better. The reason for this is the human mind is designed to default to clarity. That's what athletes call being in the zone. When we do things to force that clarity, we thwart it instead. I started to live this idea and point athletes in this direction. These athletes became successful and leaders in life, not just sports. People started seeking my advice, so I created Inner Sports twenty-two years ago.

> I never could have achieved the success that I have without setting physical activity and health goals.
>
> **Bonnie Blair**
>
> SPEED SKATER

What's the best thing about your job?

The best thing is pointing people in a direction that will help them not only on the field, course, court, or rink, but in their lives and careers as well.

What's the most challenging thing about your job?

The most challenging thing is that sports psychologists and mental coaches have turned off athletes and coaches with their quick-fix strategies and external techniques, and I often get lumped in with them. My aim is to straighten out the misalign- ment between the experience of performers when they're at their best (no thought) and the tools of performance coaches, which require the performer to think in order to be implemented.

> I think the way to become the best is to just have fun.
>
> **Shaun White**
>
> SNOWBOARDER
>
> ☆

As a kid, did you think you would have this career when you grew up? Why or why not? What were your expectations?

No! That was not in the cards at all. Even when I graduated from college, I worked in construction, not in any sports-related career.

What advice or tips can you give young people thinking of a career in your field?

If you want to have an impact on others and you love sports, this is a great career! Just remain open to the journey because you never know where it's taking you. Don't have tunnel vision. I think the quarterback on a football team is a good example. He has a plan when he is calling plays, but things don't always work out the way he expects, so he has to be able to remain open, adapt, and embrace the shifting landscape. Young people should live their lives the same way.

What demands does your job put on your personal life? How do you deal with them?

In the early days, there was lots of travel. I was away a lot and missed many of my family's activities and my children's games. However, my experiences were exciting and invaluable. Helping others is the only thing that could keep me away from my wife and children.

SPOTLIGHT

The Welsch Sisters:
The Endurance of Champions

Endurance running is a demanding sport that is meant for grown-ups. Competitors run for miles, but they don't run on a track or a road. Instead, they tackle wilderness trails and rocky paths that wind up and down cliffs, through forests, and along rivers. It's a grueling, difficult sport. Yet two sisters who haven't even reached their teens are making names for themselves in this extreme racing world.

Kaytlynn and Heather Welsch were twelve and ten years old, respectively, when they fully caught people's attention in 2013. The sisters, who are from Texas, have competed in many endurance events, including marathons and triathlons. They started running because their small size made it hard for them to succeed at other sports. Plus, they just love to run, especially along wilderness trails. Kaytlynn once complained that competing in road races was boring because, as she said in a *New York Times* article in 2012, "All you see is house, house, lamppost, lamppost." However, the girls do sometimes worry about being lost in the woods or running into a bear.

Although Kaytlynn and Heather say they love running and are determined to compete—and even dream of running in the Olympics when they are old enough—some people are worried about them. Endurance running is hard on the body, and many doctors warn that young people can damage their bones, muscles, and joints, and also affect their physical development if they push themselves too hard. Their parents have the girls checked by doctors and have gotten the medical okay for them to compete. It remains to be seen what's in store for Kaytlynn's and Heather's running careers, but one thing is for sure—they certainly are off to a flying start!

TRAINING ATHLETES

Athletic trainers specialize in preventing, diagnosing, and treating injuries and illnesses related to sports. They usually work for schools or teams and work under the direction of a physician.

An athletic trainer needs excellent knowledge of medical skills, along with health, anatomy, nutrition, and pretty much anything else that has to do with the human body. Along with having medical knowledge and the ability to use it, trainers also need to be good at making decisions and be detail oriented and good record keepers. Good people skills and excellent communication skills are also a must.

Athletic trainers generally take medical courses and get a bachelor of science degree in athletic training. Look for a program that is accredited, or approved, by the Commission on Accreditation of Athletic Training Education, or CAATE. In addition, trainers need to be certified through an exam given by the Board of Certification (BOC). This is generally done after the student has graduated. Athletic trainers also require a license and may also need a teaching license. This is a well-paid field.

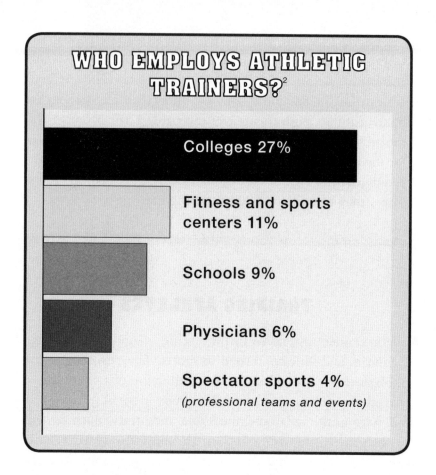

WHO EMPLOYS ATHLETIC TRAINERS?[2]

Colleges 27%

Fitness and sports centers 11%

Schools 9%

Physicians 6%

Spectator sports 4%
(professional teams and events)

BIG LEAGUE profile

Name: Danielle DeLay
Job: Athletic trainer, Clarkstown North High School, New City, New York

Why do you love sports?

I've loved sports since I was a little kid. I love competing, winning, learning from others, being part of a team. I love watching and reading about sports because there is always a common theme of excitement and work ethic, and I have a really strong appreciation for those things.

Why do you think it's important for young people to get involved in sports?

There is such a strong sense of pride and accomplishment when you achieve a goal in sports that I don't think you get quite anywhere else. The hours of blood, sweat, tears, and fighting through pain all become worth it when you win a championship or earn an MVP [most valuable player] award. I can't think of any other feeling like that. The benefits of finding something to keep you physically active are also necessary for a healthy lifestyle, which will carry over even when your playing days end.

What was your professional journey? How did you get to where you are today?

I graduated from the State University of New York at Cortland in 2010 with my bachelor of science in athletic training. From there I was hired by Mercy College and worked there for a year. I heard about the opportunity at Clarkstown North, which just so happens to be my alma mater. It was an opportunity I could not pass up and was lucky enough to get. I've been here for a little over a year and a half now and could not be happier.

What is a typical day like for you?

I usually arrive at North by 12:30 PM or 12:45 PM, in the middle of our seventh period of the school day. I use this time to answer emails, catch up on any paperwork, and file doctor's notes with our school nurses. I also use this time to set up my athletic training room for when the athletes begin to arrive around 2:00 PM, when the school day ends. The next one and a half to two hours are always chaotic, with athletes arriving in the athletic training room to perform their rehabilitation programs or to see me to have their injuries evaluated or treated. Most practices begin between 2:30 and 3:00 PM, so depending on what season it is (fall, winter, or spring), I am either driving out on my golf cart to various practice fields or walking through the buildings of our school to check in on various practices. Depending on the scheduling of practices or games, my day usually ends between 7:00 and 8:00 PM. Weekends and school breaks are usually my most hectic times, when I'll get to my office by 8:00 AM and stay until the last practice ends, which could be any time, depending on the coach's schedule.

What education did you pursue to get a job in this career? What classes were particularly helpful?
I have a bachelor's in athletic training from SUNY Cortland, and I am working toward my master's in exercise science from California University of Pennsylvania. CalU is great because it is an online program, which means I do schoolwork on my own time. The classes that were particularly helpful for my career were anatomy and physiology, biomechanics, exercise physiology, emergency management techniques, essentials of athletic training, and rehabilitation program design. All of these make up the basis of my athletic training knowledge.

What work or volunteer experiences helped you gain experience and contacts as you moved up in your career?
During the winter break of my senior year of college, I volunteered at a physical therapy clinic. At the time, I was considering the possibility of obtaining dual certification as an athletic trainer and physical therapist. Since getting the job at North, I often refer my athletes to physical therapy at the same clinic. Attending conferences and continuing education events have also been very helpful in making contacts throughout my career.

THE TRAINER'S MANY HATS

A trainer has many responsibilities:

• Prevent injuries by teaching athletes and implementing programs, as well as applying protective devices such as tape or padding

• Recognize and evaluate injuries

• Apply emergency first aid

• Develop and carry out rehab programs

• Take care of administrative tasks, such as keeping medical records and writing reports

What is the best thing about your job?
Definitely the best part of my job is watching an athlete return to play after an injury. Nothing makes me happier than seeing all the hard work that the athlete put into reha-bilitation manifest in a return to fully playing the sport that [that athlete] loves.

What is the most challenging thing about your job?
The hours are probably the toughest part of my job. Although it is wonderful to come to work around noon, this often means staying later into the night. The fact that my hours revolve around sports practices and games means that I don't get conventional vacation days, so it's difficult for me to plan vacations or long weekends away with friends and family.

Who helped you the most in furthering your career and how?
It's a tie between my high school athletic trainer, who got me interested in the profession, and my favorite professor in

college. Both were always very encouraging of me which was a huge help, mainly because at times I tend to doubt my abilities and not trust myself. I never would have considered being an athletic trainer if it weren't for my high school athletic trainer, and my college professor really pushed me to practice my skills and get better each and every day.

As a kid, did you think you would have this career when you grew up? Why or why not? What were your expectations?

As a kid, I really wanted to be a veterinarian. I have always loved animals, but as I got older, I became more interested in the human body. I knew when I chose this career path that I would be in for long hours, low pay, and minimal recognition, but the idea that I could be around sports and athletes as a career for the rest of my life made it all worth it.

What advice or tips can you give young people thinking of a career in your field?

If you are not good at time management, you need to fix that before you become an athletic trainer. Your clinical field experience is an absolutely necessary part of your education, and it will take up most of your free time. Being able to budget your time wisely so that you can fit in school, athletic training, family, and friends is very important in this career. My other tip would be to have a sense of humor. It is one of the best attributes an athletic trainer can have—it makes the stress of the job a lot easier to handle.

Do you plan to stay in your career for a long time? If not, what do you think you will do after your career is over?

As of right now, I see myself being an athletic trainer for the rest of my professional life. Things could always change, however, which is why getting my master's degree is so important. When my career is over, I think the first thing I'll do is take a long vacation to make up for all those I have missed. Then I will probably teach athletic training at a college.

What demands does your job put on your personal life? How do you deal with them?
Time is probably the biggest demand of my job and also the one that mostly impacts my personal life. It's hard to balance the hours I put in at my job with spending time with those most important to me. I'm lucky in that I almost always have one day off per week, so I try to always take advantage of that day by spending time with my friends and family. Even then, though, I miss out on some events because of my job. It's an unfortunate reality but one that I was perfectly aware of when I chose my career.

> Never underestimate the power of dreams and the influence of the human spirit. We are all the same in this notion: the potential for greatness lives within each of us.
>
> **Wilma Rudolph**
> TRACK-AND-FIELD ATHLETE

HELPING TO HEAL

A physical therapist works with patients to restore movement and flexibility after an injury. You may work in doctor's offices, hospitals, rehab centers, gyms, or for sports teams and universities. Some physical therapists work independently and visit patients in their homes. You'll need to focus on health and science in high school and college. The next step is a master's or doctorate degree in physical therapy from a school accredited by the Commission on Accreditation in Physical Therapy Education (CAPTE). Physical therapists do not need to be licensed, but it is a good idea and makes you a better job candidate.

Notes:

1. Ferguson Publishing, *Careers in Focus: Sports*, 4th ed. (New York: Ferguson Publishing, 2008), 135.

2. Bureau of Labor Statistics, "Athletic Trainers," *Occupational Outlook Handbook, 2012–2013 Edition*, US Department of Labor, accessed March 18, 2013, http://www.bls.gov/ooh/healthcare/athletic-trainers.htm

7

Sign on the Dotted Line: Agents, Lawyers, and Other Businesspeople

Are you a deal maker? Are you savvy about money? Do you love to find the best deals or come up with new angles to make money and have fun? If you have a head for business or like to make deals, a job in the business world of sports could be just the right spot for you. There are many ways to combine business with sports, from the agents who represent top athletes (and those athletes aiming for the top) to the folks who write team contracts and manage the money side of sports.

MEET MY AGENT

Athletes are focused on training and playing—they don't have time to think about getting the best deal from a team or a sponsor, or even finding a sponsor or coming up with a plan to market a product. Yet those business options are an important part of building an athlete's reputation and public image, not to mention the bank account. That's where the agent comes in.

Agents act as representatives for athletes. You conduct business negotiations; provide clients with advice; and help arrange public appearances, product endorsements, and financial investments, among other business deals. In a time when athletes have become celebrities as much as actors and rock stars, having an agent is very important. Originally, agents only handled contract negotiations, but as athletes became more well-known as celebrities and more opportunities came along for them to appear in public and sell products, the agent's role expanded to include everything from commercial endorsements to financial investments to finding a job after retirement—in short, pretty much every aspect of an athlete's business life. While an agent can work with both entertainment and sports celebrities, usually you specialize in one area.

A Day in the Life

What do agents do all day? Business deals mostly. An agent's day is usually filled with meetings and phone calls. Finding business opportunities is a two-way street. You may contact companies that are interested in your client and pitch ideas to them. Maybe the up-and-coming basketball star has a great idea for a new sneaker, or an Olympic swimmer wants to promote a line of nutritional supplements she feels helps her swim faster. Many companies come to the agent with deals, especially if the athlete is very popular. After Gabby Douglas became the first African-American to win the individual all-around event in gymnastics at the 2012 Summer Olympics, Kellogg's came calling and put her picture on the front of its Corn Flakes box for a multimillion dollar deal. Whether the agent goes to the company or the company comes to the agent, it's the agent's job to review the deal and see if it is a good fit for the athlete. If the agent, the athlete, and the company are all interested, there will be meetings and more phone calls to seal the deal.

Agents also spend a lot of time reading and researching. The agent needs to know the market and what companies will find a particular athlete appealing. The agent also needs to know what values and image each athlete represents. The agent is always looking for a good fit.

Agents get involved in contract negotiations too, so part of an agent's day might include reading or writing contracts or making changes to a contract in the works. Contract negotiations can be difficult and require excellent communication skills. The agent needs to clearly summarize important details, such as the athlete's salary and benefits. Maybe the contract specifies that the athlete will have to make a certain number of public appearances to promote the product, and the athlete wants a bonus payment for each appearance over that. The agent will suggest changes to the company, and eventually all sides will agree to a deal (hopefully!) and the contract will be signed. Agents also negotiate contracts with teams.

Agents should also have a plan for the athlete's future. Maybe you can arrange a contract that states a team player will become a coach with the team after the athlete's playing days are over. It's always important for an agent to know what the athlete wants and the best way to get it.

A typical day also includes lots of networking, or making connections, with potential sponsors. Agents go to events to meet sponsors and make connections with key players in business and in team management. If an agent makes a good impression on a

FAST FACT

The first radio broadcast of a baseball game was on August 5, 1921, on KDKA in Pittsburgh, Pennsylvania. Harold W. Arlin announced a game between the Pittsburgh Pirates and the Philadelphia Phillies.

sponsor, it's more likely that a sponsor will be interested in that agent's athlete and agree to a great offer.

Communication with the athlete is also an important part of an agent's day. A good agent–athlete relationship includes lots of connection between the two. An agent speaks to clients constantly, keeping them up to date on deals and getting their opinions on what they want to do.

SPOTLIGHT

Lydia Ko: Champion Golfer from Down Under

When five-year-old Lydia Ko walked into a golf shop with her mother, she probably didn't know that her life was about to change forever. Ko began playing golf soon after the visit, coached by Guy Wilson, who was the owner of the shop. She quickly showed everyone she had what it takes to be a champion.

Ko was born on April 24, 1997, in Seoul, South Korea. Along with her parents and a younger sister, she moved to Auckland, New Zealand, a few years later. Known as Lyds to her fans in New Zealand, she has become a popular figure in the New Zealand sports world. And she is awfully good at

what she does! Ko is currently the top-ranked woman amateur golfer in the world. In 2012, she became the youngest person ever to win a professional golf tour event, an LPGA (Ladies Professional Golf Association) event. A year later, in August 2013, she became the only amateur to win two LPGA tour events.[1]

For Ko, golf is a full-time job. She plays thirty-five hours a week and often travels to tournaments around the world.[2] Ko says the best things about playing golf are "meeting new people, enjoying competitions against different ages, concentrating on games, and seeing hard work pay off."[3] At the

same time, Ko is also a pretty typical teenage girl. She attends the
Pinehurst School in Auckland, and
enjoys drawing, reading, swimming, and playing the piano. She
also makes time for her friends.
Several of her best friends live in
Korea, so she spends a lot of time
talking to them via social media
sites, just like any teenager does!

Ko turned sixteen in 2013,
and she and her family face a big
decision: Should she turn professional? To do so, Ko would
have to get a waiver, or special permission, from the LPGA.
That's because LPGA rules say a woman has to be eighteen
to become a professional golfer. Ko can play in LPGA events
as an amateur, but she cannot claim any of the prize money.
It is estimated that Ko has lost close to one million dollars
by not playing professionally. She also can't sign any lucrative endorsement deals until she turns pro. Most observers
believe Ko will turn pro in 2013, but Ko herself has said
it is just something she, her family, and her advisor are still
considering.[4]

What has led to Ko's amazing success? She has natural talent, of course, but also the dedication to work hard. And
she has a positive attitude. In a profile written when she was
thirteen, Lydia said she looked in the mirror each morning
and told herself, "I am capable of doing absolutely anything I
possibly can reach to."[5]

The Partnership

An agent and an athlete are partners. The athlete performs well in
a sport and stays away from scandal in his or her personal life. It's

up to the athlete not only to perform well on the field but also to be a good role model off the field. An athlete with a wholesome or family-friendly image will have more opportunities than an athlete who is constantly causing havoc or getting into legal trouble. Corporations love athletes who appeal to everyone and make their brand look good. A cereal company that markets its products to kids and families isn't going to be too happy if the athlete on its cereal boxes gets arrested!

In return, the agent finds good deals that make the athlete's image shine even more. You are not going to be looking for a deal with a company that has shady business practices or sells a product that people think is unhealthy or bad. Agents have to be extremely careful what endorsements they choose for clients. The agent's goal is to make the athlete more popular and more appealing to a bigger section of the audience.

Bringing in the Big Bucks

Sports agents can make incredible amounts of money. An agent gets a percentage of whatever an athlete earns. If a top athlete earns $50 million dollars a year and the agent gets five percent of that... well, you do the math. (The answer is a cool $2.5 million for the agent.) Commissions of 3 to 5 percent are common for agents, but these percentages can go even higher. Of course, not everyone can represent a superstar, and most agents don't make anything close to $2.5 million per deal or even per year. Just as most athletes don't hit the big leagues, most agents don't either. However, for someone who is ambitious and loves sports and business, becoming a sports agent is a great idea.

So, How Do I Get There?

If you want to become a sports agent, you need to start working toward that goal in high school. Take courses in business, accounting, economics, and math to improve your money-managing skills, and take courses in English and speech to become good at negotiating and presenting a strong image to clients. When you go on to college, continue to focus on business and management. Law classes are important too.

It's also critically important to spend time with athletes. Agenting is all about making connections, and if you have a connection to a top athlete at your school or in your community, you can be in a good position to stay by that athlete's side and help that person rise to the top. Even if you don't play a sport, volunteer to work with your school's athletic teams and make yourself useful to both players and coaches. It's never too early to start networking.

Getting your foot in the door is difficult, since there aren't any professional organizations or formal courses of study to become a sports agent. Once you're in college, look for internships or entry-level jobs at sports agencies. Work hard and pass along any tips you have on hot, fresh talent, and you may be able to get a permanent job with an agency. A successful sports agent needs to hustle, and that's true of finding a job as well as representing an athlete.

RUNNING THE TEAM

Maybe your interests lie in managing a team's business rather than an individual athlete's. In that case, you might aspire to be a sports executive, such as a team president or general manager. A job in this position means you are representing and managing a sports organization, not an athlete.

Team presidents are the chief executive officers of the team. That's a fancy way of saying you are the top dog, the head honcho, the big cheese. Team presidents are responsible for the team's financial success, as well as its success on the field (although the day-to-day responsibilities for playing will lie with the team's managers). Presidents are in charge of several departments, including legal, marketing and public relations, broadcasting, advertising, ticket sales, community relations, and accounting.

A team's general manager works just under its president and is responsible for the day-to-day success of the team. A general manager handles things like hiring and firing employees (and players), supervising scouts, making trades, and negotiating players' contracts. A good general manager not only has to love and understand the sport—they must also love and understand business.

Competition for an executive job is very fierce. There aren't that many professional teams, so that means there are a limited number of jobs available. In addition, if you want to be a team president or other executive, you need to work your way up. Your first job is not going to be in the CEO's chair!

SPORTS EXECUTIVES NEED TO BE . . .

- Dynamic
- Good speakers
- Smart businesspeople
- Excellent organizers
- Good decision makers
- Well-known in the community
- Attentive to details

BIG LEAGUE profile

Name: Howard White
Job: Vice President, Jordan Brand, Nike

Why do you love sports?
Sports have taught me many valuable lessons for the game of life, such as how to be patient and have a great work ethic.

They have taught me how to be humble in victory and how to handle defeat gracefully and how to go after my goals.

Why do you think it's important for young people to get involved in sports?
Sports gives you a solid foundation around some of the core principles in life. Teamwork is huge in life. You seldom win by yourself. Practice makes perfect, and good habits pay huge dividends. And it's a great outlet. Not to mention the health benefits.

What is a typical day like for you?
A day filled with people coming by my office. I'm somewhat like Yoda! Everyone needs a Yoda in their life.

What education did you pursue to get a job in this career?
I got a degree from the University of Maryland. I majored in administrative recreation and minored in business. My leadership classes helped a lot because I was able to access my strengths and use them. Bringing people together was key. Also being able to deal with the downfalls in life. Getting over the major disappointments. Having the right attitude. Being able to adjust to the challenges of people and life. Not ever being a victim! You can always find a reason why something is someone else's fault. Being accountable and responsible for my actions.

What work or volunteer experiences helped you gain experience and contacts as you moved up in your career?
I played college basketball and then became a college coach. I left and went with the insurance industry for a while before joining Nike. My biggest asset is people. People are my business! People make the world go around, including young people—I love speaking at different functions for kids. My

mother told me when I was young, "Even a dog can wag its tail when it passes you on the street." That's what I live by.

What's the best thing about your job?
The people I meet. The people who come into my life.

What's the most challenging thing about your job?
The people I meet. Dealing with very different types of people.

Who helped you the most in furthering your career and how?
I'd say that there were lots of people who helped me, from the CEO to the janitor and everyone in between. The saying from my mother is what really helped me. The harder I work, the luckier I get.

As a kid, did you think you would have this career when you grew up? Why or why not? What were your expectations?
I thought I'd be a pro basketball player. I got injured, and fate had other things in store for me. Staying positive and humble has put me in front of great people. It's not the opportunity but what one does with each opportunity he or she gets.

What advice or tips can you give young people thinking of a career in your field?
Be able to deal with the ups and downs. Don't be afraid to fail.

FAST FACT

London is the only city to have hosted the Olympics three times: 1908, 1948, and 2012.

Those are the people who do extraordinary things in life.

Do you plan to stay in your career for a long time? If not, what do you think you will do after your career is over?
I've been with Nike for thirty years. I'm here for the duration. And then I'll write another book or two and a movie script.

> You miss 100 percent of the shots you don't take.
>
> **Wayne Gretzky**
> HOCKEY PLAYER, COACH, AND EXECUTIVE

What demands does your job put on your personal life? How do you deal with them?
Any job can be hard on your personal life. If you can't handle that, maybe it's not the job for you. If you want something out of life, you'll have to give something up to get it. Hopefully you put it in at the front end and get it back on back end. Life is give and take. Most people simply want to take from it. Just don't let that someone be you.

Getting Started

Sports is a business, so your preparation for a career as a team executive needs to focus on business and management skills. You'll want to study business, accounting, economics, computer science, English, and speech in high school.

Succeeding in business generally means having a college degree. When you move on to college, continue building on your high school courses and work toward a major in business administration or a related field. Looking past college, many executives go on to obtain a master's degree in business administration and sports administration. You need to focus on being a corporate executive, not just someone who loves sports.

> Ever bike? Now that's something that makes life worth living! . . . Oh, to just grip your handlebars and lay down to it, and go ripping and tearing through streets and road, over railroad tracks and bridges, threading crowds, avoiding collision, at twenty miles or more an hour, and wondering all the time when you're going to smash up. Well, now, that's something! And then go home again after three hours of it . . . and then to think that tomorrow I can do it all over again!
>
> **Jack London**
>
> WRITER

Of course, being passionate about sports is important too. During your high school and college days, look for opportunities to get involved in sports, especially in managerial ways. Maybe you're team captain or manager. Maybe you're the coach's assistant. Most school teams have students who keep records, chart statistics, or take charge of equipment. These are all great ways to get experience and see how athletic organizations work off the field.

Don't be afraid to look beyond your school too. Is there a minor league team in your area? Do organizations hold swim or track meets at a local college or gym? Talk to the general manager of any local team or organization and see what opportunities are available. You might start out as a volunteer or a low-paid summer employee, but you will be gaining valuable experience and a chance to see teamwork from the inside.

Sports organizations and even professional teams are always looking for interns, so this is another route you'll want to explore. Hundreds of internships are available throughout the country—the majority of sports organizations offer them. Interns are generally not paid or not paid very well, but you may be able to get academic credit for your internship. And you will be gaining experience and networking with professionals who may be able to help you in the future. If you are serious about working in the sports industry, an internship is one of the best ways to achieve your goals.

Name: Annelise Loevlie
Job: Vice President (VP), Icelantic Skis and First Degree Boots, Denver, Colorado

Why do you love sports?

Sports are an expression of who I am. They are a way for me to connect to my body and to the physical earth and also a way to feel alive! As a business owner and developer, I am oftentimes working with my head (brain) in an office with minimum physical activity or fresh air. Sports, specifically outdoor sports, allow me to get outside, move my body, breathe fresh air, feel the sun on my skin, and develop my physical body. Sports are also an excellent stress reliever and way to decompress. When I am participating in my sports, I am in the moment and thinking of nothing else. It's recreating at its prime.

Why do you think it's important for young people to get involved in sports?

Sports teach us endurance, focus, strength, strategy, competition, teamwork, and discipline, just to name a few. Through sports, we also experience victory, defeat, hard work, and the importance of persistence and practice. All of these lessons and skills can be applied to everyday life and help immensely when done so. As women, sports are important to help us become familiar with our bodies, our skills, and our abilities. With this knowledge comes body awareness, a deeply rooted confidence, and ultimately, a positive body image.

What is a typical day like for you?

I travel 60 percent of my time, so every day seems to hold new adventures to be had, problems to be solved, people to be met, and work to be done. My mornings are where I connect with myself. No matter where I am or what time zone I wake up in, I make sure to take at least an hour of me time before doing any sort of work. This usually involves drinking two large glasses of water upon waking (it gets things flowing), moving my body (running, yoga, stretching, deep breathing, walking), and a quiet sit. Additionally, I make sure to eat a healthy breakfast, usually involving lots of fresh fruits and vegetables. Other consistencies involve talking with people about various projects, a lot of meetings, and communication inside the company and outside: emails, phone calls, meetings, and creative problem solving. And the occasional sing-and-dance party when I need a release!

What education did you pursue to get a job in this career?

I have a bachelor of science degree in business administration from the University of Vermont. This was a four-year program, which exposed students to every facet of business, from finance to law, ethics to marketing. The benefit of doing this, for me, was to get exposed to every side of business and to get a feel for what I like and don't like—what I'm good at and what I should leave alone.

What work or volunteer experiences helped you gain experience and contacts as you moved up in your career?

I have always loved business. From the time I was six years old, I had lemonade stands on the corner all summer long, making and saving money to invest in certain things. I have also always loved sports and moving my body in the natural environment. My professional journey has involved everything from the restaurant industry (every position you can imagine), to sales manager for a magazine, working for an online information publishing business, to where I am today with Icelantic. The Icelantic journey began in 2005 with my best friend, Ben, who had the idea to make skis. He called on me to help him develop the business on an international level, and since then I have held every position available in the company: from bookkeeper to CFO (chief financial officer), marketing manager to ski tester—and finally to where I stand today as VP of a vibrant, growing international business.

My mom always said, "You never know until you try." This phrase has had a huge influence on me gaining both experience and contacts in my career path. This has opened several doors for me and introduced me to people I may have never encountered. Opportunities are everywhere if you are open to them, and many times they come in interesting shapes and sizes. Also, asking for help has been a huge element in my career building and personal development. People want to help and want to share experiences.

What's the best thing about your job?
The best thing about my job is that I get to work with some of my best friends, and I get to ski all over the world. The snow sports industry is a young, creative, and progressive industry with a lot of passionate participants. The fact that my job involves spreading the stoke to as many people as possible is what makes me get out of bed every day. Also, the freedom and trust with time and creativity within our company culture are amazing and suit me well.

What's the most challenging thing about your job?
Funnily enough, the freedom and trust I talked about are sometimes the most challenging things about my job. As Voltaire said, "With great power comes great responsibility." These are words I have to constantly remind myself of.

"Power" in my business basically means that I, along with Ben, my business partner, make all of the major decisions for the company. Not only do these decisions affect our coworkers, but also our brand message, product quality, distribution channels, sales numbers—potentially everything in the business. So even though we have the freedom or power to make anything happen, there is a lot of groundwork and follow-through that must be in place for things to survive.

> All sports for all people.
>
> **Pierre de Coubertin**
>
> FOUNDER OF THE INTERNATIONAL OLYMPIC COMMITTEE AND ACADEMIC

Who helped you the most in furthering your career and how?

I have been blessed to be surrounded by an amazing family and community with endless experience, knowledge, and ears that listen, and I have called on many of those at various times in my life. Of everyone, though, Ben has helped me the most in furthering my career. Ben and I have been friends since we were eleven years old (twenty years now!), so we have both seen and experienced a lot about each other and about life. Because we work so closely together, he challenges me more than anyone else to be myself—an important challenge in personal and career development. He also teaches me things about business and life by being himself.

As a kid, did you think you would have this career when you grew up? Why or why not? What were your expectations?

I always knew that I would have my own business and that it would involve traveling and something fun, like skiing. I never knew specifics, but I've always loved the idea of affecting the world throughout business and sports. Funny how things pan out!

What advice or tips can you give young people thinking of a career in your field?

Ski! If you want to get into the ski/snowboard/snow sports industry, the most important thing you can do is to participate in the sport. This is an industry of lifestyle—there is, in general, not huge money in it, but that is not why people are here. By pursuing your passion and developing yourself through adventures and experiences in the sport, you will find where you fit in. So get out there and remember, you never know until you try.

Do you plan to stay in your career for a long time? If not, what do you think you will do after your career is over?

I plan to always be associated with Icelantic and the ski industry. Whether I will hold the same position is unknown. I have no immediate plans to leave, and I intend to continue listening to my heart and following the signs that have led me to where I am today. I trust that these will take me where I'm going next.

What demands does your job put on your personal life? How do you deal with them?

I travel a lot, which is awesome most of the time but also hard on certain aspects of life. Being home for brief intervals makes it hard to maintain relationships, routines, health, and any sort of consistency in my personal life. Though it makes it more challenging, it is still very possible, and with the time I do have at home, I am very present, and I spend it with my very special friends. Also, with my health, I have learned what my body needs in order to operate optimally. Food, sleep, and exercise are three main focuses for me, and though my efforts are not perfect, they are excellent for the amount of demands I place on myself.

EVERY TEAM NEEDS A PLACE TO PLAY

You can manage an athlete. You can run a team. Or you can run an entire stadium! That's what sports facility managers do, and this can be another exciting career for someone who wants to combine a love of sports and business.

Sports facility managers (also known as stadium or arena managers or stadium operations executives) are the people who handle the day-to-day operations of a sports facility. These folks get to plan everything about the place people and teams play, from buying or leasing the facility to designing and constructing it so it's just right for the team or sporting event involved. Sports facility managers also supervise the grounds, buildings, and all the people who work there.

If You Build It . . .

Some sports facility managers handle the day-to-day operations of an existing facility. Others are in charge of building a facility first. When a team or a school decides to build a stadium or a gym for public sporting events, there are many details to consider. The sports facility manager might be involved in finding a site for the building, buying or leasing the land, and building a facility or redesigning an existing building to meet the needs of the organization. The manager needs to understand local zoning laws, which govern what can be built and how the building can be used, as well as other federal or state rules for construction. The manager also needs to understand the neighborhood. How will a sports facility impact traffic in the area? What about noise levels? Residents may welcome a sports facility to their neighborhood, but they are also going to be very concerned about noise, pollution, traffic, and crowds. The sports

> The goal is to keep having fun. Not let that pressure get to me and still be Missy.
>
> **Missy Franklin**
>
> SWIMMER

facility manager is one of the people who works with the community to make sure the facility is welcome there and benefits the residents.

MODERN SPORTS FACILITIES ARE LIKE MINI-CITIES!

Take a walk around a stadium or other sports facility, and you may be amazed at how many different things you'll find there. There's the playing field, of course, and the seats for spectators to watch the excitement. There are also:

Practice areas

Home and visiting team locker rooms

Physical therapy areas

Sports equipment storage

Maintenance equipment storage

Press boxes and press rooms

Restaurants and bars

Food vendors

Offices for business executives and staff

Public areas, such as the concourse

Lots of restrooms

Play areas for children

Pretty much everything else you need for players and fans to enjoy themselves!

Once a stadium is built, the facility manager's next job begins. You are in charge of hiring staff, including security, or contracting with an outside company to provide these services, and making sure the grounds are clean and neat, all public areas are safe and appealing, and the teams and athletes have what they need to play well. Even little things can be a big problem. For example, what if the vendor who provides paper goods fails to show up? If spectators have no cups to drink their sodas or no napkins to wipe the mustard off their faces after a hot dog, they are not going to be happy.

As the manager, you may work in an office, but you need to understand and be a part of all areas of the stadium. You also need to be aware of what's going on with employees and people in the facility. Do the food vendors have what they need to operate safely? Are the spectators having a good time? Is everything clean, neat, and working correctly? If not, how can the problem be fixed? The sports facility manager has to see the big picture and be aware of every little thing going on in the building or facility.

A CLOSER LOOK

The oldest college program in sports administration and facility management is located at Ohio University in Athens, Ohio. The program is administered by the Center for Sports Administration, which is part of the university's Department of Sports Administration Academic Programs. The program requires fifty-five credit hours (including an internship) and includes courses in business administration, journalism, communications, management, marketing, sports administration, and facility management. Graduates of this program emerge with a master's degree in sports administration, not to mention lots of valuable experience that can pay off in a job offer. You can learn how to get more information about Ohio University's program in chapter 11.

How to Prepare

Like becoming a sports agent or a team executive, becoming a sports facility manager requires lots of business and communications skills, as well as a college degree. People who are interested in this sort of job generally focus on business and math classes in school, as well as classes in government, speech, and writing. Outside the classroom, managing a school club or other organization can help you see the responsibilities involved, such as handling money or delegating responsibility. Internships and volunteer opportunities are other great ways to make connections and gain experience. Once you get a job with a facility, look for ways to advance from an entry-level position to jobs with increasing levels of responsibility.

Certification in facility management is not required at this time, but it is very good to have and shows you are a step ahead of other candidates for a job. The International Facility Management Association and the International Association of Venue Managers, Inc., both offer programs that lead to certification.

Sports facility management is a demanding job, but it pays well. Certification can lead to higher salaries. According to the International Facility Management Association, its certified members earn an average of 13 percent more than noncertified workers in the same field. You can find more information about certification in chapter 11.

HOW DO YOU MANAGE EQUIPMENT?

Somebody has to keep track of all those bats and balls, helmets and hockey sticks, hurdles and tape, right? Why not you? A sports equipment manager is responsible for maintaining, ordering, and inventorying athletic equipment and uniforms. Most of them work for college and high school teams, but professional teams employ these managers too.

Athletes can't play without uniforms, safety equipment, and the other tools of their trade. Not only do these things need to be available and ready to use by game time, but they also need to be in good condition and safe to use. According to the Athletic Equipment Managers' Association (AEMA), once plastic shell football helmets were introduced, the game got rougher and injuries became more frequent. To prevent injuries, it is essential that football helmets fit properly. A group called the National Operating Committee on Standards in Athletic Equipment developed standards for football helmets. Trainers and coaches soon realized that it was important other types of equipment fit properly as well. The AEMA was formed in 1974 to address these concerns.

Since the formation of the AEMA, the responsibilities of equipment managers have become more diverse and vary depending on where the manager works. A typical job description includes ordering all equipment, making sure uniforms and equipment fit properly, inspecting and cleaning equipment (even doing laundry!), and inventorying and storing equipment when it isn't being used. Equipment managers may also come up with budgets and must know all the rules regarding uniforms and equipment.

This is a job for someone who has good organizational skills and an eye for detail. Good communication skills are a must too. The sports equipment manager should also have good people skills, since you will be working daily with coaches, players, and managers.

If this sounds like a career for you, your high school courses should include business, math, and computer science. Volunteering as the equipment manager on your school's teams is a big plus too.

The AEMA has specific guidelines for education after high school. They recommend one of the following paths: 1) a high school degree and five years of paid, nonstudent employment in athletic equipment management; 2) a four-year college degree and two years paid, nonstudent employment in the field; or 3) a four-year college degree and at least 1,800 hours as a student equipment manager. The AEMA also has a certification program, which can make a potential manager more desirable to employers, and the organization offers scholarships to students as well.

Don't be afraid to start at the bottom and work your way up. Terry Schlatter, the head athletic equipment manager at the University of Wisconsin–Madison, recalled, "I started out doing laundry, then went to fitting shoes and helmets. Then I was responsible for ordering all of the football equipment. From there, I became head equipment manager and was responsible for ordering equipment for all the sports."[6]

Notes:

1. Matt Richens, "Lydia Ko Wins Second Straight Canadian Open," Stuff.co.za, August 26, 2013, www.stuff.co.nz/sport/golf/9086996/ Lydia-Ko-wins-second-straight-Canadian-Open.

2. The website of Lydia Ko, accessed September 9, 2013, www.lydiako.co.nz/ profile.

3. Ibid.

4. Randall Mell, "Debate Over Lydia, 16, Turning Pro Ko-tinues," GolfChannel.com, August 31, 2013, www.golfchannel.com/news/ golftalkcentral/ko-family-considering-deferred-waiver-16-year-old-lydia.

5. The website of Lydia Ko.

6. *Careers in Focus: Sports*, 92.

8

Coming to You Live: Broadcasters, Writers, and Photographers

Words are powerful things. Although sports are games of action, words, whether spoken or written, do a remarkable job of capturing the excitement, drama, triumph, and sometimes tragedy of athletic events. If you have the gift of bringing action to life through your writing or your voice, think about a career in reporting or announcing. And if you're handy with a camera, a career in sports photography might be for you.

ANNOUNCING VS. BROADCASTING— WHAT'S THE DIFFERENCE?

Do you have a way with words and a voice that makes people stop and listen to you? Is your vocabulary colorful, dramatic, and visual? Then think about a career as a sports broadcaster.

Sports broadcasters (or sportscasters for short) work for radio and television stations, writing and delivering footage of current sports news. Sportscasters might appear on the nightly news or on special broadcasts of sporting events. Along with providing play-by-play descriptions during a game or event, sportscasters often appear on air before and after the event, interviewing coaches and athletes and providing highlights of the action.

Sports announcers, on the other hand, work for teams as the official voice of a team. If you've ever attended a sporting event, you've heard someone make pregame announcements, player introductions, and a detailed description of the game, including who has scored or incurred a penalty, who is substituting for another player, or when there is a timeout. These announcers keep everyone informed.

SPOTLIGHT

Walt Frazier: A Star on the Court and in the Broadcasting Booth

During the early 1970s, few players were as admired as Walt "Clyde" Frazier. The guard for the New York Knicks had style both on and off the court and was especially known for his flashy talent at stealing the ball and setting up plays. "It's Clyde's ball," one of his teammates, Willis Reed, said to *Sport* magazine. "He just lets us play with it once in a while."

Frazier was born in 1945 and grew up playing basketball on the broken-down playground court of his segregated school in Atlanta, Georgia. He moved north to attend Southern Illinois University on a basketball scholarship. Frazier quickly became one of the best college basketball players in the country. He was selected by the New York Knicks as the fifth pick in the 1967 NBA draft. In 1970 and 1973, Frazier led the team to their only NBA championships.

Frazier retired from basketball in 1979. He was elected to the Naismith Memorial Basketball Hall of Fame in 1987 and named to the list of 50 Greatest Players in NBA History in 1996. After living out of the country for a few years, he returned to New York in 1989 to try a new career: broadcasting. Frazier became a commentator for Knicks' broadcasts on the MSG Networks. His language was as flashy as his playing had been, and soon the air was filled with "Clyde-isms"—clever rhyming phrases that perfectly described the action, such as "dishing and swishing," "duping and hooping," and "bounding and astounding." Through his broadcast work, Frazier gained a new generation of fans.

WHAT'S SO GREAT ABOUT BROADCASTING?

You get to interview athletes, coaches, and other team personnel.

You get an inside look at sports and the people involved.

You get to attend games and other sporting events.

You get to appear on television or radio.

You get to meet all sorts of interesting people.

You get to be the center of attention (well, sort of).

You can become known to audiences around your town or around the world!

Prepare to Be on the Air

For many sports broadcasters, the day starts long before an event or interview. You need to know what you're talking about, so you spend most of your time doing research and gathering background information on subjects. For a sportscaster, those five minutes on the air are usually preceded by hours of work.

As an announcer, you do most of your work during the game or event, but you need to prepare as well. Announcers need a strong knowledge of the game, its history, its rules, and its statistics so you can keep the audience informed and provide background information for what's going on down on the field or court. You need to be able to create visual pictures, especially if you are being broadcast over the radio, so an ability to speak clearly, think fast, and be creative is a big plus.

ADVICE FROM A PRO

John Earnhardt of the National Association of Broadcasters recommended: "Write about your school's sports teams for your school newspaper or hometown newspaper and read, read, read about sports. Knowledge about the area you are interested in reporting about is the best tool for success. It is also necessary to be able to express yourself well through the spoken word. Speaking before an audience can be the best practice for speaking before the camera or a microphone."[2]

How do you prepare for a job in sports broadcasting or announcing? As with most careers, it's best to start while you're in school. High school has many classes that will prepare you. Most important are classes that will improve your speaking and writing skills, such as English, speech, journalism, drama, and even foreign languages. Most broadcasters have a four-year college degree, usually in communications or journalism. During both high school and college, look for opportunities in your school and community, such as writing for the school or local paper or announcing on a school or local radio or television station. Of course, you should know sports inside and out as well and have an outgoing personality, a great memory, a good speaking voice, and a sense of fun and adventure.

Most sportscasters are employed by television networks or radio stations. You may reach an audience of millions or a few thousand, depending on the market. Announcers can work for universities, high schools, and professional teams in both the minor and major leagues.

The Sound of Your Own Voice

Many sportscasters audition by making an audiotape or video-tape of themselves describing a particular sporting event and sending this tape to potential employees. Try this for yourself. Watch a game live or on TV and create a video or audiotape of yourself broadcasting the action as it happens. You may not use this tape to audition for anything, but it is great practice—and a lot of fun too!

A Huge Range of $$$

Salaries for sports announcers and broadcasters vary widely, and that's an understatement! Announcers for a small minor league team or at school sporting events might be paid by the game. Full-time announcers and broadcasters have a salary, and those in small markets make a lot less money than broadcasters on national networks or those working in big-city markets such as New York or Los Angeles. If you throw former pro athletes and sports celebrities—many of whom go on to announcing careers after their playing days are over—into the salary mix, the sky's the limit. Many celebrity broadcasters bring home millions of dollars a year.

FAST FACT

The first televised sporting event in the United States was a college baseball game between the Columbia Lions and the Princeton Tigers, broadcast on NBC on May 17, 1939.

Name: Adam Bjaranson
Job: Studio host, Portland Trail Blazers; television sports anchor and reporter

Why do you love sports?
Sports have always been a huge part of my life. I grew up in the Bay Area, California, and was quickly introduced to all sports. I played soccer as a child and attended many professional sporting events in Oakland/San Francisco. My dad was the major influence. He didn't force any sport on me, but his passion for the A's (Oakland's baseball team), Raiders (Oakland's football team), Warriors (Oakland's basketball team), and Seals (San Francisco's ice hockey team) was second to none. That has stuck with me to this day. While I've worked in the sports profession for a couple decades now, I'm still as much of a fan today as I was in my preteen years.

Why do you think it's important for young people to get involved in sports?
You always hear about sports being a diversion from some of the more serious things that kids today take part in. Sports are great on so many social levels. You build fast friendships that can lead to future business relationships. Plus, competition is healthy in helping mold kids. Being part of a team is great, but individual sports are also. A motto that I've always lived with in the sports profession is this: It's not how good you are—it's how good you want to be. That tends to keep the fire burning. After all, everybody—whether in sports or not—wants to be liked, right?

What is a typical day like for you?

I need to know as much about the fifteen players (and their opponents) as possible. You can never be too informed. Since I only work on game nights (yes, that's only eighty-two nights a year), I want to be as prepared as possible. I peruse the game notes for any useful information, meet with the show producer, and decide what information is best for our viewers. My partner on the show is a former Trail Blazers guard, Michael Holton. He handles analyst duties. I like to always have bullet points in front of me. Some nights, we'll meet with season ticket holders prior to our show for a Q&A session. Also, there are quite a few team functions that the team requests we attend. This past season also allowed me to do some radio work and host our online magazine show, *Trail Blazers Courtside*. The radio show, *Trail Blazers Fifth Quarter*, is a caller-driven show where fans can call in and talk about the game, ask questions of us, etc.

What education did you pursue to get a job in this career?

I got a bachelor of science degree in speech communication from Portland State University. I also took some theater classes. These both helped me become a better public speaker. When you are in the public eye, there are always going to be schools, charities, etc., that would like you to speak at various events.

Internships were the best way for me to learn. There is no experience like experience itself. Fortunately for me, I was able to work at KPTV as an intern in the sports department long before I was hired there. It was invaluable to me. So I always encourage anybody to find those internships. They are great tools to have.

> Success is where preparation and opportunity meet.
>
> **Bobby Unser**
>
> AUTOMOBILE RACER AND COMMENTATOR
>
> ⭐

What work or volunteer experiences helped you gain experience and contacts as you moved up in your career?

While playing sports in high school, I always wanted to become a professional baseball player. But the truth was I wasn't that good. So I decided if I couldn't play sports, I wanted to be able to talk about sports. It was then that I decided this was my true calling in my professional life. So I attended Portland State University and got my degree in speech communication. After that I decided to move back to California and fine-tune this career. I began as an intern with the Golden State Warriors alongside the team's radio play-by-play guy (Tim Roye). I did this while going through the College of Extended Learning at San Francisco State University (SFSU). While in the sports broadcasting program, I was able to do play-by-play of the school's basketball and baseball teams. I also did stories at Raiders Training Camp and a new ad campaign for the Oakland A's. These were all the teams I grew up loving. I was hooked. From there I put together demo tapes. And boy, are those fun to look back on these days.

I was very determined to eventually find my way back to Portland, Oregon. So after sending out about twenty tapes for various openings across the country, I landed my first job as the sports reporter at a small CBS news bureau (KCBY) in Coos Bay, Oregon. Sadly, the money was very little. You've got to pay your dues, as they say, but after three months cutting my teeth, I couldn't keep doing it financially. I moved back to the Bay Area. After seven months of trying to get back into television, I got a call from the news director at KVEW-TV (an ABC affiliate) in the Tri-Cities, Washington (the towns of Pasco, Richland, and Kennewick). They had an opening for a weekend sports anchor. The news director

Sport is a preserver of health.

Hippocrates
GREEK PHYSICIAN

had one question for me: "Why should I take a chance on you after you left your last job after just three months?" The only thing I could tell him was this: "Giving my word is the only thing I have right now, but I won't disappoint you. And you have my word on that." Thankfully, he gave me that shot. I stayed there until October of 2001.

At that point, I felt I was seasoned enough to try getting to Portland. It would be a jump of about one hundred television markets. The only position available was as sports photographer. I was also up for a sports director job in Champaign, Illinois. So I had a decision to make. Head to Portland, taking an off-air position, or go to a market that I didn't know a thing about. I decided to take on what was familiar to me. After three months at KPTV in Portland, I began filling in as the weekend sports anchor while a couple guys were on vacation. And the rest is, well, history. Right place at the right time. I worked at KPTV (FOX) as the weekend sports anchor from October of 2001 until December of 2004.

Then KPTV was slicing back on sports and cut me down to thirty-two hours a week. Colin Cowherd (now at ESPN) was leaving his job at KGW (NBC) in Portland. That station did sports right, always had. And I loved its product, even though it was my competition then. I decided it was time to make a run at KGW. I hired an agent to get me from KPTV to KGW. That was my dream job. Plus, there was no noncompete clause in play. They could get me right away. Sure enough, things worked out and I was hired as their sports reporter. Eventually I moved into the main seat and stayed there from 2004 until

> The thing you learn from sports—setting goals, being part of a team, confidence— that's invaluable. It's not about trophies and ribbons. It's about being on time for practice, accepting challenges, and being fearful of the elements.
>
> **Summer Sanders**
>
> SWIMMER AND COMMENTATOR

2010 when the Portland Trail Blazers recruited me away. They had a position that I felt was just to my liking: television studio host. They had me when they said, "You get the summers off." Who wouldn't want that? I helped launch their digital network too, hosting a show each morning. Then on game nights, my role was to host the thirty-minute pregame, half-time, and postgame shows. It's the position I still hold today. Dream jobs in my dream city. It doesn't usually happen that way, but I consider myself very fortunate.

The broadcasting business is a very tight-knit fraternity. Along the way, you run into so many colleagues and former classmates. It's imperative to never burn any bridges in this business. If you do, the word spreads like wildfire, and you'll be at the unemployment office before you know it. My mom always taught me to treat other people like you want to be treated yourself. I have always used that trait to forge ahead in the world of broadcasting. Also, it's best to never use the word *can't*. At every stop, I've had the pleasure of working alongside many quality broadcasting professionals. I've kept them close along the way too. Some have been huge mentors to me, and even close friends. Always ask teachers and professors for references. They are the lifeblood of helping you move forward.

What's the best thing about your job?
The best thing about my job is the people I come in contact with. It doesn't matter if they are coworkers or viewers. It never gets old getting to talk sports with them. I always strive to do the best job possible. Being in front of hundreds of thousands each game night is a complete rush. But not nearly the rush you get from somebody who says, "I love watching your show. You do a great job." That's about as rewarding as it gets for me.

What's the most challenging thing about your job?
The most challenging part of my job is still adjusting to no teleprompter. For the better part of fifteen years, that was my

security blanket. The words are always there. I still try to memorize a few things, and that can get me into trouble. All of it is what comes at the top of your mind. So you have to think on the fly quite a bit. Aside from that, having summers off has turned into a challenge. I'm one of those rare breeds that just likes to work year round.

WORLD'S HIGHEST PAID ATHLETES IN 2012[2]

1. Floyd Mayweather (boxing) $85 million winnings

2. Manny Pacquiáo (boxing) $62 million winnings and endorsements

3. Tiger Woods (golf) $59.4 million winnings and endorsements

4. LeBron James (basketball) $53 million salary and endorsements

5. Roger Federer (tennis) $52.7 million winnings and endorsements

6. Kobe Bryant (basketball) $52.3 million salary and endorsements

7. Phil Mickelson (golf) $47.8 million winnings and endorsements

8. David Beckham (soccer) $46 million salary and endorsements

9. Cristiano Ronaldo (soccer) $42.5 million salary and endorsements

10. Peyton Manning (football) $42.4 million salary and endorsements

Who helped you the most in furthering your career and how?

I don't think there was one single person who helped most, but there are two guys who gave me some perspective in how to approach this business moving forward. Dennis Patchin (KXLY-Spokane, Washington) and Val Sakovich (SFSU professor). They were always encouraging me and cheering me on. I always think of them when I think of this broadcasting path I've carved out. They were both instrumental in my early television years.

As a kid, did you think you would have this career when you grew up? Why or why not? What were your expectations?

Yes, I was determined to become a sportscaster in Portland. We moved to Oregon when I was eight, and I always thought that that looked like a fun job. Find something you love to do, and it will never seem like work. I never dread a single day of having to go into work. My expectations of myself are to be the best that I can be. And to this day, I've never felt like I've reached my true potential. I'm constantly striving to improve and that will likely never change.

What advice or tips can you give young people thinking of a career in your field?

The best advice is this: accentuate the positive and eliminate the negative. I fully realize that thousands of broadcasters would die to have my job. I don't take it for granted at all. It's turned into a profession of "it's not what you know—it's who you know." So make as many contacts as possible in your chosen field. I've realized that people are willing to help out, as long as you are dedicated. Also, when sending out your demo reels, don't be discouraged. Keep plugging away at it. You'll be told no on more than one occasion. But eventually you'll be able to achieve what seemed like the unachievable.

Do you plan to stay in your career for a long time? If not, what do you think you will do after your career is over?

I'd love nothing more than to stay in this field forever. It's funny when I think about what I do. My job is to talk about what athletes do right or what they do wrong. That's it. But no day is the same. There are incredible stories out there to be told. If I ever got out of this profession, they'd have to force me out. Or I'd have to win the lottery. And I'm not so sure that would even push me out.

What demands does your job put on your personal life? How do you deal with them?

In my personal life, this profession doesn't really have a lot of challenges. I met my wonderful wife when she was a producer at KPTV, so she understands the demands. But there are times when my buddies have a golf trip planned, and I've got a game that night. Again, when you work just 82 nights out of 365 in a year (not including preseason or playoffs, which would make it no more than 100), life is good. Just find something you enjoy and pursue it. It's a wonderful world once you get in. Best of luck to all the aspiring journalists out there. Whether for on camera or off, there are many creative minds that this industry craves.

WHAT IS MEDIA RELATIONS AND HOW CAN I GET A JOB IN IT?

Media relations is a field related to broadcasting. A media relations specialist combines broadcasting knowledge and ability with experience in public relations. Public relations is the art of making a person or a company look good, so media relations specialists make sure clients get good press in every medium. Basically, these specialists serve as a link between the athletes or team and the broadcasters, reporters, and other media folks who want to write about them. Media relations specialists can work for public relations agencies, sports agents, teams, and universities.

TO GET A JOB IN MEDIA RELATIONS, YOU NEED TO:

- Be a great speaker and writer

- Have good business sense

- Have great communications skills

- Get along well with people

- Take high school classes in English, speech, debate, communications, business, and computers

- Get a bachelor's degree in communications, journalism, public relations, or marketing

- Work on publicity or ad solicitation for school and club events, such as the yearbook, a dance, or a fundraiser

- Work at your school's radio or television station or on your school newspaper

- Intern to gain experience and make contacts

- Get accredited by the Public Relations Society of America or the International Association of Business Communicators (see chapter 11 for contact information)

- Talk to your college counselor about career opportunities in this field

- Gain work experience by starting out in a general public relations career

- Create a file of your media clippings and other work you do to show future employers

Most media relations specialists work in an office and at athletic events and media showcases. Competition for jobs in this field is stiff because it is a desirable and seemingly glamorous career.

Name: Mike Sheridan
Job: Director of Media Relations, Villanova University, Philadelphia, Pennsylvania

Why do you love sports?
As a young person, I was attracted to the excitement and incredible performances I saw from professional and college athletes. My father is a big sports fan, and we watched a lot of games on television together. I was also fortunate to be exposed to baseball, soccer, and basketball through Little League and community recreation leagues, which further developed my interest in sports. As a player, you pick up on some of the nuances of the sport that enhances your connection to it.

Probably the biggest hook came when I attended my first professional sporting event. It was a baseball game at Shea Stadium when I was ten that I still have vivid recollections of. A year or two later, I saw my first NBA game at Madison Square Garden and loved the whole scene: the crowds, the noise, rooting for the home team. It's a spectacle.

All these years later, that excitement is still there. Plus, in this position, I still get to be part of a team and experience all the highs and lows that come with that, even though I am not out there competing. The aspect of teamwork is very rewarding.

Why do you think it's important for young people to get involved in sports?

To me, the most valuable thing young people get out of sports is the sense of teamwork. The best teams in any sport are often those for whom the sum is greater than the individual parts. Whenever I ask some of our alumni in different sports what they miss most about their athletic experiences, the most common answer is the camaraderie and friendships.

I also believe it's important that young people gain an appreciation for exercise at a young age. Even if they don't necessarily love sports, it's extremely valuable to develop an appreciation for maintaining a healthy body—it's incredibly helpful to create that feeling as a younger person rather than trying to build that appreciation as an adult.

What was your professional journey? How did you get to where you are today?

By the time I reached high school, it was apparent that I would not have the skill level to compete against the best of my age group in any sport. At both Albertus Magnus High School and Fordham University, though, I found a way to stay connected to sports through writing at the school paper and in college also working at the student radio station (WFUV). Those experiences helped me land a position at a national basketball and baseball publication based in Michigan when I graduated college. I spent fourteen years as a managing editor and columnist at *Basketball Times* and *Baseball Bulletin* before transitioning to the university side of things at Villanova in 1998. I have been the director of media relations in athletics since 2002, with men's basketball and men's soccer as my primary sports.

What is a typical day like for you?

During the months of September through April, when our athletic seasons are in full swing, the workdays are very full. The basketball team usually plays two games a week, and we have a host of other in-season events—twenty-four varsity sports with full schedules of home and road competitions, coaches' radio shows, and banquets—that require our attention and sometimes include travel outside this area. Fortunately, we have a great media relations team.

In the summer months, when none of the university's athletic teams are in season, the pace is more restrained. We have more time in the office and more hours to devote to long-range projects and planning.

One man practicing sportsmanship is far better than a hundred teaching it.

Knute Rockne

FOOTBALL COACH

What education did you pursue to get a job in this career? What classes were particularly helpful?

I received a communications degree from Fordham and took a number of journalism and television courses while at Rose Hill. All were helpful in some form. However, the most impactful experiences I had and contacts made came via extracurricular work at the radio station and college newspaper. There, I was exposed to the importance of deadlines and learned the basics of how to construct interesting stories.

What work or volunteer experiences helped you gain experience and contacts as you moved up in your career?

When I entered the business, I was fortunate to land at a small sports publishing company that allowed me to get a taste of every element of the business, from publishing to sales to covering events like the World Series and Final Four. I also learned layout and design, which still serves me well to this day.

I also made some valuable contacts through recreational softball. There was a press club team in Detroit that helped introduce me to members of the media in my adopted city.

What is the best thing about your job?
The best part of my job is the interaction with the student athletes and the coaches who mentor them. There is an incredible energy that comes with it and a very rewarding sense when former students return as well-rounded, success-ful professionals in fields in and out of athletics. You feel like you, in some small way, may have contributed to their lives.

I also like watching the games unfold, whether they take place in a packed twenty-thousand-seat arena or on a quiet field with a few dozen spectators. I enjoy seeing athletes excel and in my time at Villanova have been fortunate to watch a lot of spectacular performances.

Finally, it's very rewarding to be part of a community like the one we have here at Villanova. The downside of working in a small company is that there is a tiny group of two to three people in your daily work area. Here, you have a wide cross section of people you come in contact with every day, and it's a part of this that I very much appreciate.

What is the most challenging thing about your job?
Probably the management of time. The pace can be hectic when your teams are having success as you attempt to serve multiple masters in the media and internally. Those are excit-ing times and where all of us in this profession want to be. But they also require us to serve as a buffer so that the coaches and, most important, athletes aren't overwhelmed by media requests. It's important that we manage those requests so that our athletes can focus on being students too.

Who helped you the most in furthering your career and how?
The two individuals who stand out for me are Larry Donald and Jay Wright.

Larry was the man who hired me in 1984 and served as the editor and publisher of *Basketball Times* during my ten-ure there (he died in 2000). I learned valuable lessons about basketball and what it took to direct a successful business in that atmosphere. At a young age, I was afforded incredible freedom as a writer and visibility within the basketball community.

Jay Wright has been the head basketball coach at Villanova since 2001. Coach Wright is a tremendous ambassador for our university, in addition to being a winner of national and Big East coach of the year awards. His vision for his program and understanding of the full scope of our university and its athletic mission is truly impressive.

Lessons he offers to his team apply to anyone at any stage of life. He uses the term *attitude* to remind the athletes on his team to stay positive and upbeat—you cannot control what happens to you, but you do control how you respond to it. Being around that approach on a daily basis for twelve years has helped keep me focused on the value of remaining upbeat and enthusiastic.

There have been a number of other individuals who have been helpful too, including professors and classmates from my days at Fordham, like my friend Jimmy Smith (of *Newsday*); colleagues here at Villanova, like athletic director Vince Nicastro, and from *Basketball Times*; journalists such as Dick Weiss of the *New York Daily News* and Dan Wetzel of Yahoo! Sports; as well as public relations executive Ray Carson of the American Cancer Society.

As a kid, did you think you would have this career when you grew up? Why or why not? What were your expectations?
Like most sports-loving kids, I probably was more focused on what it would feel like to become a player at the highest level than what it might be like to write about sports or serve as a member of the administrative team. But I do believe that if you had told the ten-year-old me that this is where he would end up, having been able to live a life in sports, I am confident he would have been pretty thrilled.

What advice or tips can you give young people thinking of a career in your field?

The best part about a life in sports is that it features people who are truly passionate about their career. In my experience, people don't typically fall into a career in sports as they do some others—they choose it because it thrills them.

The simplest advice I can offer to those interested in pursuing this as a career is to start wherever you can. If you aren't an athlete, perhaps you can help a team at your school as a volunteer manager helping the coaches. Teams in junior high and high school can often use a student eager to be involved. Sometimes all you have to do is ask—the coach may have you keep score or help at practice. It won't be glamorous, but it can be a start.

Later, that opportunity could come via an internship or a volunteer position at a student publication or radio station. It might not be in exactly the kind of sport you know best. But if you jump in with energy and enthusiasm for helping the team and organization you are a part of to succeed, the opportunity to advance will find you.

Do you plan to stay in your career for a long time? If not, what do you think you will do after your career is over?

I would hope that I have the chance to remain a part of the athletics world for years to come. I have been at it for twenty-eight years professionally and am as enthused about it now as I was in 1984.

Right now, I don't view myself as a full-scale retirement type of person. I realize that day may come. But my hope would be to continue with some kind of active role—perhaps through freelance writing, consulting, or other forms of part-time work in athletics— into my golden years.

What demands does your job put on your personal life? How do you deal with them?

I am blessed to work at a university and basketball program that very much value the role of family. As much as possible, we are able to include our spouses—and children if you have them—in team functions and other aspects of campus life. My wife, Kristin, attends many of our home basketball games, and we have had the opportunity to bring our nephews and nieces to summer camps and give them a chance to meet some of the athletes they have seen on television. It also helps to have an understanding wife who appreciates my passion for this profession and university.

What is your salary or compensation?

I have never spent a lot of time considering how my salary compares to others in the industry. I have a position I enjoy at a great university, and that's what matters most to me.

SPOTLIGHT

Elliott Almond: All-Around Sports Guy with a Focus on Giving Back

Elliott Almond has played sports since he can remember, but he hopes his legacy will be in giving back and in writing.

Inspired by his father, an excellent tennis player, Almond made his high school varsity team as a freshman. He lettered in basketball, tennis, cross-country, and track and field in high school, but gravitated toward beach volleyball and surfing for his teens through his thirties. In 1983, he and his friends caught a one-hundred-year swell from the island of Todos Santos off Ensenada in Baja, California. In doing so, they "discovered" one of the West Coast's now-famous big waves. Almond is the author of the book *Surfing: Mastering Waves from Basic to Intermediate*, but he considers the most profound moment of his surfing career to be when he rescued a man caught in a huge surf from drowning.

A three-time nominee for the Pulitzer Prize and veteran of the *Los Angeles Times*, *Seattle Times*, and *San Jose Mercury News*, Almond has worked long and hard for his love of sports writing, starting in high school. As a junior he covered local sports for his small-town weekly. After accepting weekend and night assignments at various newspapers while he earned his bachelor's degree in communications (minor in political science), he worked at the *Los Angeles Times* for twenty years, moving up from being a copy editor to being an investigative sports writer covering big stories on drugs before the 1984 Olympics.

He loves his job because he sees it as an honor to tell the stories people trust him with. He seeks to instill that ethic and passion in student journalists and does that in part by speaking with high school classes and through his work as co-managing editor of Mosaic, a two-week high school journalism boot camp. He and his colleagues hope to make the program a year-round nonprofit to support schools that don't offer journalism anymore.

A WAY WITH WORDS OR IMAGES

Maybe you like to write but aren't really interested in being on the air. That's fine! There are plenty of opportunities to share your feelings, opinions, and knowledge about sports with the world. You can be a news reporter, a columnist, a blogger, or a book author, to name just a few career paths.

People who write about sports can work for a specific company. For example, a sports reporter might work for a newspaper—anything from the local paper to a national paper like the *New York Times* or *USA Today*. Reporters also work for magazines—again, anything from a local mag to a top market one, such as *Sports Illustrated*. There are also sports magazines that cater to specific sports, such as *Baseball Digest*. And there are sports and media websites that employ writers, columnists, and bloggers to inform and entertain their readers.

SO, HOW DO YOU BECOME A WRITER IN THE SPORTS WORLD?

IN HIGH SCHOOL

- Take English, journalism, writing, and computer classes.
- Write for your school paper or magazine.
- Develop your research and writing skills.

IN COLLEGE

- Get a bachelor's degree in English, journalism, or communications.
- Write for your school paper or magazine.
- Find an internship in a journalism or writing-oriented field.

ANYTIME

- Start a blog or create a website.
- Promote your site and yourself through social media.

Many writers also work as freelancers. A freelancer gets assignments from different companies and is not on staff for only one company. You are paid by the article rather than receiving a salary. The benefits of freelancing are that you can make your own hours, accept projects that interest you so you can write about what you want, and work from home. The downside is that you do not have a regular income, especially at first, and you don't receive any benefits such as health insurance or paid vacations. You are, in essence, your own boss, so you're responsible for everything your boss would normally provide.

If you're interested in photography, the employers and fields open to you are pretty similar to those for writers. Jobs are available at newspapers and magazines as well as at pro teams and at universities with large athletic departments. To prepare for this field, you'll want to take photography and journalism courses in high school and college and get experience volunteering for your school newspaper, magazine, and yearbook. Look for opportunities in your community as well. When it comes to creative careers, you're never too young to start honing your talent and gaining experience.

Name: Brock Landes
Age: 13
Job (when not studying!): Baseball, basketball, and football player, Murray Avenue School and Huntingdon Valley Athletics Association, Huntingdon Valley, Pennsylvania; blogger, www.themlbnation.com and www.MLBBOARDS.com
Dream Job: Sports broadcaster

What sports have you participated in and when?

I have been playing baseball, basketball, and football since I was very little. I have been going to sports broadcasting camp for four years.

What are you doing now in terms of education/sports participation?

I play on both school teams and township teams. I have attended Play by Play Sports Broadcasting Camp for four years. I have a YouTube channel where I post videos showing off my sports card collection, which I buy and trade through YouTube. I have also met friends from all over. I even have a friend from Guam! I have several blogs that I write on daily. I watch sports channels, mainly MLB Network, and I do research on up-and-coming players on the internet.

How did you get started in sports?

I have been hearing about sports and the arguments associated with sports since I was old enough to understand what my father was talking about. My father, a sports fanatic, introduced sports to me when I was very young. At the age of four, I began playing baseball and basketball. A few years later, football started for me. In between my sports, I started collecting sports cards, which keeps me connected with stats, attributes, and players. I also get a lot of information from my father about the history of sports.

What do you like best about sports?

I enjoy playing, learning how to deal with failure, and learning how to get along and work with my teammates. I enjoy the debates that sports generate between people. Last, but certainly not least, I enjoy the friends I have made through sports.

Do you plan to stay in sports for a long time?

Yes, I hope to make a career out of sports broadcasting or even have a radio talk show. With everything I've learned at sports broadcasting camp, it seems like an awesome profession to enter. I now write blogs and articles for themlbnation.com and mlbboards.com, and I write about numerous baseball topics. I hope to one day fulfill my dreams of becoming a sports broadcaster or sports writer. I hope to enter the profession of sportscasting via television, radio, etc. I am willing to work as hard as it takes to pursue my dream. Participating in sports broadcasting camp has been extremely helpful for me in deciding what I would like to do further down the road. Through camp, we learn how to anchor, talk sports, debate, and almost anything along those lines, which has helped me in ways I can't explain. Writing and talking about sports come easy to me now.

What advice or tips can you give young people thinking of a career in sports?
Do everything you can at a young age because, if you do, you have a lot of time to learn and progress. Be personable, play as many sports as you can, and watch as many sports as you can. Learn as much as you can, any way possible, because the more research you do and the more information you obtain, the more knowledgeable you become with sports. Get your name out there as well. You know, write on websites, make package videos, comment on articles— basically anything to stay involved with sports and the passion for sports talk.

Picture It!

Use what you have. The most used type of camera in all of history is the cell phone camera. It may be all you have on hand when you attend a sporting event. How can you take amazing photographs of great moments with the camera you carry in your pocket?

Compose well: Imagine a tic-tac-toe grid on top of the scene. Set elements of interest not along the lines but at the intersections.

Capture movement: Hold the camera phone with both hands and move the camera at the same speed as the subject. This will make the subject appear clear to the photograph's viewer and will blur the background.

Anticipate shutter lag: Get used to your camera phone's timing so when something interesting happens, you'll have a good feel for the point when you need to press the button.

Name: Abe Asher
Age: 16
Job (when not studying!): Sports writer, Oregon Sports News and EPL Talk, former sports blogger @abesworldsports
Dream Job: Writer

Talk about your blog. How did you get started? How do you get your information? What do you like to blog about?
I started my website in November 2010 through Google Sites, a free, easy, painless way to create a website. I wanted to fuse my love of sports and a growing passion for writing into one place where I could share and archive my thoughts. I get most

of my information through first-hand experiences watching games or reading the newspaper or other online resources. There is so much sports knowledge and opinion readily available, there is no shortage of info. I like to write about soccer, specifically the Portland Timbers, and college football, specifically the Oregon Ducks. I also like to explore social and political issues in sports and dive into different stadium experiences in many different sports.

What sports have you participated in and when?

I've played baseball, basketball, soccer, and tennis. I played soccer all my life until high school and baseball until around the start of middle school. I currently play varsity high school tennis and JV basketball.

What are you doing now in terms of education/sports participation?

I'm a high schooler in Portland, Oregon, and I play tennis and basketball for my school.

How did you get started in sports?

I got started in sports on my dad's lap, watching the 2001 World Series. It was one of the best World Series of all time, the New York Yankees and the Arizona Diamondbacks. Play was emotionally charged due to the harrowing attacks of September 11th, and on the field it was a thrilling, seven-game tug-of-war, with walk-off home runs, bloopers, and history at every turn. I was only four at the time, but the stakes and intensity and wonder of that World Series catapulted my life in sports.

What do you like best about sports?
I love the theater of sports. It's the best kind of reality television. It's real, it's hard, it's joyous. Sports are a kind of alternative universe going on in the midst of our usual universe—there are good guys and bad guys, teams and events, rules and regulations, politicking, scandal, characters left and right. I also love the games themselves—what humans can do in an athletic setting—and I love the feel of sports. There is nothing as exciting as being in a sports arena during a big game. The energy is unmatched. All over sports we see unbridled emotion—sports are well and truly alive.

WHAT'S THE DIFFERENCE?

A *sports reporter* tells the facts and describes a news or sporting event.

A *sports columnist* reports news stories but adds personal opinions, style, and experiences to the story.

A *sports blogger* is like an online columnist, commenting about news stories or informing readers about important events.

A *sports author* writes books about sports, athletes or other sports personalities, or sporting events.

Do you plan to stay in sports for a long time?
I think sports will always be in my life in some way. Who knows if I will be in the sports industry, but through playing sports, watching sports, and being around sports, I will always have sports as a part of my life.

What are your career goals and dreams?

I want to become a professional writer. I'd love to write columns, and it'd be great to stay in Portland.

What advice or tips can you give young people thinking of a career in sports?

I'd tell people considering a career in sports to remember why they love the games. To remember how to be a fan, to never lose sight of what makes sports fun. Cynicism is poison. No, the sports world isn't a fairy-tale kingdom—it's full of cheating, drugs, back-door deals, and mediocrity—but through all of that, sports is a truly magical place to spend time. Don't ever forget that.

Notes:

1. Ferguson Publishing, *Careers in Focus: Sports*, 4th ed. (New York: Ferguson Publishing, 2008), 84.
2. "The World's Highest Paid Athletes," *Forbes*, June 2013, http://www.forbes.com/athletes/list/.

9

Think Outside the Box: A Few More People Who Work in Sports

The previous chapters covered a lot of sports careers, but there are still more that don't fit under the categories we've already discussed. So, if you haven't found your perfect job yet, fear not! This chapter presents a few other career options.

ARCHIVIST OR HISTORIAN

An archivist acquires and preserves historical documents, objects, artwork, photographs, and other things. If you've ever gone to a sports museum and seen a contract signed by a famous athlete, the tennis racquet used by a player at Wimbledon, or a baseball from the World Series, you've seen the work of an archivist firsthand.

Archivists work closely with historians. The archivists focus on the objects that bring the event and the people involved to life for spectators in today's world; historians focus on the story— the what, where, when, why, who, and how of an event. Archivists and historians also work to catalog items. In this role, you may take photographs or make copies and save the information on a computer and number each item so you know what you have and where it is. Archivists also repair damaged items and provide an appraisal, or value, of an item.

Museums and libraries are the biggest employers of archivists. Some large universities also have collections of memorabilia. Museums often buy or receive donations of items from private collectors and either exhibit them for a short time or keep them for their permanent collections. In the sports world, there are many museums and halls of fame dedicated to specific sports— everything from baseball to swimming to track and field and much more. All of these places employ archivists and historians.

If you are interested in an archival career, your best bet is to focus on history, library, research, and English courses. When you move on to college, continue to study history or library science. Many colleges and universities have museums that can provide you with experience or allow you to create your own major or minor in museum studies. To get a job as an archivist or historian, you will most likely need a master's degree in history or library science. The Academy of Certified Archivists provides a certification program in archival work.

Getting a job as a sports archivist or historian is tough. There are few openings in the field, and many people who work in sports museums or halls of fame are volunteers or part-time employees. The pay isn't great even for full-time employees. Budget cuts are expected to lower both pay rates and opportunities in the field. However, there will always be opportunities in archiving and sports history—you just need to be creative, flexible, and determined to find them.

Name: Sondra Novak
Job: Visual Merchandiser and Project Manager/North America Sales Go-to-Market Operations, Nike

Why do you love sports?
The feeling of being a part of something bigger than yourself and that each game/day is a new beginning where anything can happen no matter what happened the day before.

Why do you think it's important for young people to get involved in sports?
It teaches children a lot of valuable lessons, including how to work as a team, responsibility, the value of hard work, and how to accept and move on from disappointment or loss. I also think it helps build self-esteem and confidence, which are very important skills to have in life and are much easier to develop early.

What is a typical day like for you?
I don't really have a "typical" day in my job, which is one of the things I like the most. But my day usually consists of one of the following scenarios:
- If I am not working at an event, I spend my day attending meetings about upcoming events and projects that I

am working on, and working at my desk on the details of the various events that I have coming up. This can vary from putting floor plans together to ordering and pulling product that needs to be displayed.

- If I am setting up an event, I am pulling product, dressing mannequins, setting walls, and making sure that everything looks the way it is supposed to.
- If I am working at an event, I am one of the first ones there, making sure everything is set up and ready to go for the day's meetings, and one of the last to leave, making sure everything is cleaned up and secure for the night.

What education did you pursue to get a job in this career?

I have my BA in psychology and elementary education. When I graduated, there weren't many teaching jobs available so I had to look for work elsewhere. I worked at Nike and enjoyed it during high school and breaks from college, so I went back to that. I have found that my classes helped me learn how to identify and work with different types of personalities and that has helped a lot with what I am doing now.

What work or volunteer experiences helped you gain experience and contacts as you moved up in your career?

I started working at Nike backstage at fashion shows when I was fifteen because my aunt needed extra help. I continued to work there when I could during high school and on breaks from college. Through that, I met some people who needed help doing room setups and visual merchandising. They taught me the basics on the job, and I continued to learn more

> Sports do not build character. They reveal it.
>
> **Heywood Broun**
>
> WRITER

techniques and skills along the way. I was willing to work hard and do anything that was asked of me. I was also very willing and eager to learn new things. Other people noticed and started asking me to work more on different projects. When I graduated from college, I couldn't find a full-time job, so I called my old contacts and told them I would be willing to help again whenever they need it. Through that, I met more people, and an opportunity came up to help manage a sample line and take on new projects. My role has slowly evolved and changed into a project manager/visual merchandiser.

What's the best thing about your job?
Each day is a little bit different, so I never get bored and I never fully know what to expect. This keeps me on my toes and has taught me a lot about being flexible and creative. I am also blessed to work with a great team. We all have the same goal at the end of the day, and that is to do our jobs the best we can and make each event or meeting the best it can be. Having people around you with similar goals and desires helps, especially on the difficult and long days.

What's the most challenging thing about your job?
Learning how to successfully work with different types of people, especially under tight and critical deadlines.

Who helped you the most in furthering your career and how?
Outside of my family, who have always been a great support system and motivated me to explore all of my options no matter what, there are two people who have impacted

me and my career the most. They were the footwear and apparel sales directors for the [Michael] Jordan brand when I met them (they have since moved on to other jobs). I met them at a large managers' meeting on the road and offered to help them. They were so used to having to do everything on their own that they welcomed the help and were very appreciative. We got to talking about my job, and they told me that I should contact them to talk further. I did, and they gave me a lot of good tips on the next steps and introduced me to some more people at Nike. Because of them and the contacts they gave me, I started working with the Jordan team more and my opportunities and experience have grown a lot.

As a kid, did you think you would have this career when you grew up? Why or why not? What were your expectations?

I thought I was going to be a teacher until I was about twenty-four or twenty-five years old. This job was never really on my radar, so I didn't really have any expectations going in. It wasn't until I started doing it on a more regular basis that I realized that I could actually see myself doing this for a living. I didn't understand all of the planning and work that had to happen before the meetings even start until I was involved with it. That's when I started seeing it as a career possibility and not just a way to pay my bills.

Strategy gets you on the playing field, but execution pays the bills.

Gordon Eubanks

MICROCOMPUTER INDUSTRY PIONEER

What advice or tips can you give young people thinking of a career in your field?

The best advice I can give is to start talking to people. Find people who are in roles that you are interested in and ask them about their journey. It is surprising to hear the journeys that people have taken to get to the roles that they are in.

Also be willing to learn and do anything. If you have the opportunity to volunteer or work in something that is even kind of close to what you might want to do, take it. And when you get the opportunity, work hard and find ways to go above and beyond. If you do the extra things without being asked, it will get noticed. Always be willing to work hard and learn something new because this type of job is always evolving and changing, and if you aren't willing to evolve with it, you will have a much harder time being successful.

Do you plan to stay in your career for a long time? If not, what do you think you will do after your career is over?
I plan on staying in my role for a while. I am lucky that I am in a position to change and challenge myself within the role that I have. I continue to meet with people and talk to people to learn what other opportunities may be out there because I am curious and I enjoy learning new things, but I am very happy with my job the way it is for now. I don't completely know what the future holds for me and my career, but I kind of like that.

What demands does your job put on your personal life? How do you deal with them?
The biggest demand that it puts on my life is the time it takes. Working at Nike is not a nine-to-five, five-days-a-week job. It is not unusual to work a twelve-hour day during our busy times, and I often have to travel and/or work on the weekends. There are certain times in the year that, unless I work with you, I probably won't see or talk to you for a few weeks at a time. My friends and family know this and are good about it. They know that when I don't respond or can't make it to a birthday party or gathering, it's not because I don't want to—it's because I can't. To deal with it, I try to make time for friends and family in the weeks before I know that I am going to be busy and let them know when the craziness

will be over. A good thing about my job is that if I am not in the middle of a big project, I can take some time off pretty easily, whether it is by working from home, leaving early, or completely taking the day off. It's important to enjoy the time off when you have it because that is what recharges you and puts everything in perspective.

BICYCLE MECHANIC

If you're a cycling enthusiast, you know that having a bicycle in top condition is essential for safety, fun, and performance. That's why bicycle mechanics, who keep bikes in good working order, are so important. Most work for local bike shops, large sporting goods stores, or bicycle manufacturers. Others work at resorts that feature outdoor activities.

Bicycle mechanics need good technical and mechanical skills. These mechanics must pay careful attention to detail, have good hand-eye coordination, and be good at using a wide variety of tools. Because there are so many different brands and types of bicycles, bike mechanics must be familiar with lots of different characteristics and mechanical problems. You also need to be able to spot problems and fix them, identifying even minor problems before they become serious trouble. If you work in a store or at a resort, you should also have good people skills, since you will most likely be working as a salesperson or clerk and giving advice about what type of bike to buy or rent.

You don't need a degree to become a bike mechanic, but education is always a good idea. In high school, classes in physics and technical subjects will help you understand how things work and how to fix them. These classes will also train you to work with your hands, follow instructions, and understand design and mechanics. Business and communications courses can help you if you end up working in a store or other customer-oriented business.

You might want to take courses at a technical or vocational school or community college. There are also training schools specifically for bicycle mechanics (see chapter 11 for details). These schools offer certificates that can help a potential bicycle mechanic land a job.

You can also gain experience by working on your own bike and those of your friends and getting a part-time job at a bike shop or sporting goods store while you are still in school. As for pay, most workers are paid by the hour.

STACK IT!

Sports are not always about sweating; at their heart, sports are recreation, a diversion from everyday life. Sports stacking, the rapid stacking and unstacking of cups, fits this definition perfectly! Here are descriptions of a few competitive stacks:

The 3-3-3 Stack: Cups are up stacked and down stacked from left to right or right to left in three stacks made up of three cups in each stack.

The 3-6-3 Stack: Cups are up stacked and down stacked from left to right or right to left in three stacks made up of three cups on the left, six cups in the center, and three cups on the right.

The Cycle Stack: A sequence of stacks combining a 3-6-3 stack, a 6-6 stack, and a 1-10-1 stack, in that order. Stackers conclude the cycle stack with cups in a 3-6-3 down stacked position.

Doubles: Two stackers work together to complete the cycle stack, one using only the right hand while the other uses only the left hand.

PERSONAL TRAINER

Do you like working with individual athletes? Do you like the idea of devising a fitness plan that will specifically benefit that one person? Then a career as a personal trainer might just be what you're looking for.

Personal trainers assist people with exercise, weight training, rehab, and diet and nutrition. A trainer meets with a client at the client's home or the trainer's studio or health club employer for several sessions and creates a personalized exercise program to specifically address the client's concerns. Personal trainers must get a complete health history from a client and work with the client's doctor if that person is doing rehab or exercising to recover from a specific injury or illness.

To become a personal trainer, you should concentrate on physical education, health, nutrition (such as family and consumer science), and science courses during high school. English and speech classes will help improve communication skills, and business classes can help if you think you want to own your business. A college education is not required, but many personal trainers do study health education, athletic training, sports science, health, or physical education courses at a level higher than high school. You can look into associate degrees from two-year community colleges or technical schools. In addition, many personal trainers take classes in dance, yoga, and martial arts, and incorporate these techniques into their training.

It's also important for personal trainers to be certified. The best certifications are given by the American Council on Exercise, the National Federation of Professional Trainers,

FAST FACT

The world's first live televised sporting event was the 1936 Summer Olympics, which were held in Berlin, Germany. Of course, at that time, very few people had television sets.

or the American Fitness Professionals & Associates. (See chapter 11 for information on how to contact these organizations.)

There is a wide range of salaries for personal trainers. Some charge by the hour.

Inside the Belly of the Beast: A Mascot Quiz

Mascots entertain the crowd and keep everyone cheering for the home team, but it's the big scorers who get the attention. Test your knowledge about these hardworking and unique unsung heroes.

1. Can being a mascot help you get into college?
   A. Yes, it looks interesting on the application.
   B. Yes, mascots can earn scholarships at some universities.
   C. Yes, both of the above.
   D. No, it's just a fun activity.

2. What is the most common high school mascot?
   A. Eagle
   B. Tiger
   C. Hawk
   D. Bear

3. What are the mascot rules?
   A. Never reveal your human identity in public.
   B. Mascots are allowed only nonverbal communication.
   C. Mascots are not supposed to interact with other teams' mascots. If two mascots stage a "fake" fight, the home mascot is supposed to win.
   D. Mascots should not pick up babies.
   E. All of the above.
   F. Only A and B.

4. Has one of the most famous college mascots, the Notre Dame leprechaun, always represented the school?
A. Yes.
B. No, it once was a four-leaf clover.
C. No, it once was a Blarney stone.
D. No, it once was an Irish terrier.

5. Which mascot was removed by its school's administration and then reinstated after a landslide in a student vote?
A. University of Iowa Hawkeyes
B. Evergreen State College Geoducks
C. University of California Santa Cruz Banana Slugs
D. Harvard University Crimson/John Harvard

Answers
1. C. The University of Mississippi and the University of Texas at Arlington are two schools that offer assistance to mascots.
2. A. The eagle is the most common mascot for both high schools and colleges.
3. E.
4. D.
5. C. Initially chosen to represent the school's fun and inclusive spirit, the banana slug was replaced by the sea lion in 1980. Only six years later, the slug was back by popular demand.

FAST FACT

The first Winter Olympics were held in 1924.

Name: Spencer Slovic

Age: 17

Job (when not studying!): Captain, boys cross-country and track teams; Aardy the Aardvark school mascot, Oregon Episcopal School, Portland, Oregon

Dream Job: My career dream doesn't necessarily include running, but if I found a way to combine my loves uniquely and interestingly (such as making a film on runners), I would include athletics in my professional life.

What sports have you participated in and when?
Cross-country and track and field, ninth through twelfth grades; baseball, third through eighth grades; basketball, fourth through tenth grades; school mascot, occasionally over the years.

What are you doing now in terms of education/sports participation?
Entering my senior year of high school, I'm the captain of the boys cross-country and track teams. I run every day and practice with the team twice a week during the summer. I have a 4.0 GPA and got a perfect score on the SAT, but from time to time like to put on our Aardy the Aardvark mascot costume and entertain the crowd during an important home soccer or basketball game. In a school that has kids ranging from pre-K to twelfth grade, I think it's important for there to be an aspect of unity and school spirit throughout the age range, and I think our unique mascot is a way of doing that.

When kids I meet from other schools find out that my school's mascot is an aardvark, they think it's either a really awesome or a really dumb mascot. Either way, our mascot is recognized and remembered. For a small school in a big city, our mascot is a way for people to recognize and remember who we are as a community. Just as the aardvark is a unique, interesting mascot, our school community is unique, interesting, and special.

How did you get started in sports?

When I was in third grade, my gym teacher wrote in a comment that I needed to work on my catching and throwing skills. My dad started to play catch with my brother and me, and gradually we improved, joined a team, and moved into other sports. My family is composed of a lot of distance runners, and eventually I found that I liked to run too. I started off my freshman year of high school as a mediocre, just-fast-enough-to-make-varsity kid and have improved to the point of being on the all-district second team last year.

What do you like best about sports?

I probably won't become a professional athlete, but playing sports has taught me valuable lessons about how to improve myself and live life to the fullest. Team sports helped me learn to communicate and work together with other people. Running non-competitively puts me at ease, clears my mind, and helps my concentration and focus. Training for track and cross-country has given me a clear, definite example of how the amount of effort you put into something affects what you get out of it. Training for and running races has been almost like practice for other pursuits in life: studying

> I am building a fire, and every day I train, I add more fuel. At just the right moment, I light the match.
>
> **Mia Hamm**
>
> SOCCER PLAYER

for school, learning another language (I study Mandarin), improving my filmmaking skills, etc.

Do you plan to stay in sports for a long time?

I plan on being a lifelong athlete. My goal as a runner is to be one of the people who shows up for races throughout his thirties, forties, fifties, sixties . . . as long as I can. Sports might not necessarily be the central part of my life, but it will be a pursuit and habit I will always carry with me. I would rather keep running into my old age than be a superstar athlete when young and have that part of my life fade into memory. I most likely won't run for a varsity collegiate team, but I would love to be on a running club or at the very least active on intramural teams in college.

What advice or tips can you give young people thinking of a career in sports?

Hard work pays off and is necessary. Don't become discouraged that the work you put into your sport isn't paying off—gratification is delayed but well worth the wait. I made huge improvements in my last two years of high school after barely improving as an underclassman. Part of improvement is learning *how* to improve: how to work hard and push yourself to the fullest for the most gratification in your athletic pursuits.

> The score never interested me, only the game.
>
> **Mae West**
>
> ACTOR

HEALTH CLUB OWNER OR MANAGER

If you want to combine a love for physical fitness with a knack for running a business, think about a career as a health club owner or manager. These professionals own and operate fitness facilities and handle the day-to-day operations of the club. Health clubs may be part of a national or international chain or may be independent, local businesses.

In high school and college, take classes in business, accounting, health, communications, advertising and public relations, computers, and physical education to improve your communication and business skills. Volunteer or get a part-time job with a school sports team and at a health club so you can gain management skills and experience in the health or fitness industry. Certification from the International Facility Management Association (see chapter 11) may help your club have more prestige, which will lead to more clients, which will lead to a higher salary for you.

11 RESPONSIBILITIES OF HEALTH CLUB OWNERS AND MANAGERS

1. Plan fitness programs and classes

2. Check exercise equipment and make sure it is in good repair

3. Do safety checks of equipment and in classes

4. Hire teachers, trainers, and other staff

5. Supervise staff

6. Arrange special events

7. Supervise the facility so it is clean and safe

8. Keep up with safety standards and health requirements

9. Keep a budget

10. Advertise the business to get new clients

11. Create appealing membership packages for clients

FITNESS DIRECTOR

If you're interested in working at a health club but don't necessarily want to run a business, think about becoming a fitness director. Fitness directors organize and schedule classes and programs for health clubs, as well as for cruise ships, resorts, and corporations. As when you run a whole health club, when you manage a department, you must be detail oriented, coordinating schedules and offering activities that will benefit a wide range of people.

Fitness trainers should take classes in health, nutrition, physical education, and science. Participation in sports teams or clubs is a big plus! Associate's and bachelor's degree programs in health education, sports science, and athletic training will provide the necessary training and credentials, as will a certification in fitness or exercise science. (Contact the American Council on Exercise or the American Fitness Professionals & Associates for more information on certification; you can find their contact info in chapter 11.)

SPOTLIGHT

Shaun White:
Daredevil on a Board

When Shaun White was born in California in 1986, he had a serious heart condition that required several operations. No one expected White to grow into an extreme athlete, but that's exactly what happened. And he showed his talent and determination at a very young age. His family moved east, and White grew up around the ski areas of Vermont. However, by the time he was six years old, he had switched from skiing to snowboarding. This was a smart move because White was a natural at flying over the slopes on his board. White received his first sponsorship when he was just seven years old. He went on to win gold medals in the 2006 and 2010 Winter Olympics and thirteen gold medals in the Winter X Games between 2003 and 2013.

But snowboarding isn't White's only talent. He is also a wiz on a skateboard! Skateboarder Tony Hawk met White at a skatepark when White was only nine years old, and Hawk became the boy's mentor. His guidance helped White, who turned pro when he was seventeen years old. White's rewards include five medals for skateboarding in the X Games (two gold, two silver, and one bronze) as well as many other championships. He also has many endorsement deals, including deals for several snowboard and skateboard manufacturers, Oakley sunglasses, Red Bull, Target, and HP.

10

Where Do I Go from Here? Getting Started in Sports

You've read the book. You've explored the careers. You've been amazed and inspired at the huge variety of job options for people who love sports. You're sure that a career in sports is the way to go. Now what? How do you make that dream a reality? Whether you want a career as a professional athlete or one managing a team, whether you have a dedication to healing injured athletes or enforcing the rules, there are steps you can take right now to start your journey toward the career of your dreams.

SCHOOL

Those six hours a day or more you spend in school aren't just time away from playing video games and hanging with your friends.

They are the first stepping stone to your dream career. Maybe you don't love every class, but most classes can help you in a sports career. Here's how:

- Sports is an international pastime, so learning a foreign language or two will help you communicate with a wider variety of people.

- Writing essays and book reports will teach you valuable skills in expressing yourself and communicating with others.

- Math and business courses are a must for anyone. This goes for athletes interested in making the most of earnings during and after an athletic career—hoping to manage athletes, teams, or any other sports-related business.

COLLEGE COURSES ARE THE BACKBONE OF A CAREER IN SPORTS

- If you're looking to work in broadcasting or journalism, you'll probably spend a lot of time in the English or communications department.

- Medical fields require a strong science background.

- Business administration is the place to be for management jobs. Really, everyone can benefit from a good business or economics course.

- Agents and others interested in a business career should also take law classes.

- Everyone also can benefit from good public speaking and writing skills as well, so take advantage of those classes as you work your way toward your degree.

- Aspiring sports agents should study law as well as marketing and business.

- Biology and chemistry labs are essential to someone who wants to train athletes or go into a sports medicine career.

Most jobs today require a college degree. Unlike high school, college is a time to zero in on career-specific classes. Look for a school that offers the programs you want and that is a good fit for your dreams, personality, and ambitions. Do your research before you commit to a college, and you'll be happy in the long run. If at first you don't find the perfect school for you, it's never too late to transfer.

Remember, in both high school and college, your guidance counselor or career counselor is a valuable resources. Meet with that person often!

> If you think you can't, you won't, and if you think you can, you will. When I'm tired at practice, I tell myself that I'm not tired, and I can push through. If you tell yourself you're tired or if you tell yourself you're sick, your body is going to follow the mind.
>
> **Kellie Wells**
>
> TRACK-AND-FIELD ATHLETE

INTERNSHIPS

Internships are an amazing way for people, especially students, to get their foot in the door of their chosen field. An internship is generally unpaid in terms of money, but there is no replacing the experiences you'll have and the people you'll meet. Here are some of the great things you can achieve doing an internship:

- Get experience in the field you want to work in.

- Find out if your dream career is as good as you thought it was.

- Learn the basics of the industry from the ground up.

- Meet people already working in the field who can be valuable references and mentors, and provide wonderful further networking opportunities.

- Gain experience to put on your résumé, which can help you get a full-time job.

- Have the chance to go to industry events or meet celebrities or well-known business people.

- Get hands-on experience that you'd never get in the classroom alone.

SPOTLIGHT

George Steinbrenner: An Owner with a Sense of Humor and Serious Savvy

A powerhouse team should have a powerhouse owner. That was certainly true of the New York Yankees and their long-time owner, George Steinbrenner.

George Steinbrenner was born in Ohio on July 4, 1930. His family owned a profitable shipping company. While studying at Ohio State, Steinbrenner assisted the legendary football coach Woody Hayes. Later, Steinbrenner assisted the football coaches at Northwestern University and Purdue University.

Steinbrenner joined the family business in 1957 and later bought the company. After he became successful, Steinbrenner began investing his money in teams. His first purchase was the Cleveland Pipers, who played in the American Basketball League (ABL). Steinbrenner hired John McClendon, the first African-American coach in professional basketball. However, both the team and the league had financial troubles, and the ABL collapsed in 1962 after just two seasons.

On January 3, 1973, Steinbrenner and other investors bought the New York Yankees from the media company CBS. For the next thirty-three years, Steinbrenner became one of the most well-known and talked-about owners in sports. He became famous for firing—and sometimes rehiring—managers and other team officials. During his first twenty-three years of ownership, he changed managers twenty times. One manager, Billy Martin, was fired and rehired five times! Steinbrenner's iron control and huge financial support helped the Yankees, however. The team was the World Series champ for three straight years (1998, 1999, and 2000). In 2009, the Yankees won the World Series again, notching their seventh win under Steinbrenner's leadership.

Steinbrenner also had a sense of humor about his image and reputation. He made fun of himself in several commercials, hosted an episode of *Saturday Night Live* and, most famously, was a recurring character (although his part was played by an actor) on the hit television series *Seinfeld*.

Steinbrenner retired from active control of the team in 2006, leaving his two sons to manage the day-to-day ownership of the Yankees.

FAST FACT

Melbourne, Australia hosted the 1956 Olympics, but the horse-riding events were held in Stockholm, Sweden, because Australia had very strict rules about bringing animals into the country. This was the only time an Olympics was held in two countries at the same time.

Steinbrenner's health began to fail, and he died on July 13, 2010, the morning of the All-Star Game. He is still remembered today as one of the most powerful men in sports.

VOLUNTEER WORK

Volunteering for a local organization or team is a great way to gain experience and also meet people who love the sport as much as you do. Some places for volunteering include:

- School teams

- Local or community teams

- Professional sports teams or organizations

- Teams that play for or hold events to raise money for local charities

- Sports-related businesses

- Sports museums

- Stadiums, gyms, or other sports facilities

How can you find out about volunteer jobs? The best way is to contact the team or organization directly and tell the staff you're interested. Also, some foundations that hold sports-themed fundraisers will advertise for volunteers in social media or in newspapers. It's also a good idea to ask around. The more people who know you are interested in volunteering, the better your chances are of finding a position.

Name: Samantha Pearl Kaner
Age: 12
Job (when not studying!): Champion softball pitcher

What sports have you participated in and when?

I've played baseball since I was five years old, playing with the boys until fourth grade, including one year of travel with the AAU (Amateur Athletic Union). Then I switched to softball. I played Little League and travel softball for grades four through six. I played tennis competitively for three years but now, because of my commitment to softball and pitching, I only play tennis recreationally and will try out for the high school team this August.

What are you doing now in terms of education/sports participation?

We are first allowed to play school sports in the seventh grade, so I will be trying out for the high school tennis team in the fall, the middle school basketball team in the winter, and hopefully the high school softball team in the spring. I also am a straight-A+ student, play the trumpet, and am on the student council.

How did you get started in sports?

I started for fun with my friends when I moved to Suffern (New York) when I was four years old. I joined everything from soccer to basketball to Little League so I could make new friends.

What do you like best about sports?

I like the competition, but most of all I love my teammates. That's why I ended up choosing basketball and softball as my two main sports even though I may have been the best at tennis.

Do you plan to stay in sports for a long time?

Oh my gosh, yes! My goal is to play Division I college softball, and I really hope softball becomes an Olympic sport again so maybe one day I can make the Olympic Team.

What advice or tips can you give young people thinking of a career in sports?

Work hard! I started pitching so late compared to other girls, but I practice every day and work so hard, and now I am even better than most of the girls who started before me. Last summer my Little League All-Star team actually won the whole Eastern Regional Championship, and I pitched the final championship game. It was the most amazing feeling. I was even in the newspaper all the time, but most of all I am glad I spent the summer with the most amazing twelve girls, who became some of my best friends, and I will always love them and never forget the best summer of my life.

SPEEDY SPORTS[1]

Here are some stats on speed from the world of sports:

- Motorbikes race up to 360 miles per hour.

- A Formula One car can go up to 257 miles per hour. By contrast, the winner's average speed in the world's first car race, run between Paris and Rouen, France, in 1894, was just over 11 miles per hour!

- China's Fu Haifeng's powerful hit once sent a badminton shuttlecock flying at 230 miles per hour.

- Speed skiers can hit 150 miles per hour, while bobsleds zoom around the course at 90 miles per hour.

- Tennis pro Andy Roddick can serve a tennis ball at 155 miles per hour. The Williams sisters, Venus and Serena, have long dominated on the women's side of tennis with serves reaching nearly 130 miles per hour.

- Several baseball pitchers have achieved pitches over 100 miles per hour. As of the start of the 2013 season, Nolan Ryan holds the official record with a 108-mph pitch thrown in 1974.

- Want to fly over the water? Try wind surfing, which can reach speeds of 60 miles per hour.

- Racing bikes can reach speeds of almost 50 miles per hour.

- A thoroughbred racehorse gallops at 40 miles per hour.

- A human sprinter runs 23 miles per hour. Olympic champion Usain Bolt has briefly hit 30 miles per hour in races!

NETWORK, NETWORK, NETWORK!

We can't say enough about the importance of networking. Every person you come in contact with could be the person who sets you on the next step of your professional sports journey. So make friends with coaches and members of local sports organizations. Connect with people in the field you're specifically interested in. For example, if you're interested in broadcasting, make connections with the DJs at your local radio station. Be helpful, respectful, polite, and eager, and you'll make a good impression.

> What I love about the game is that the game doesn't know who is supposed to win.
>
> **Sue Enquist**
>
> COACH

SPOTLIGHT

Steven Purugganan: Up Stacking and Down Stacking His Way to Victory

He's held a Guinness World Record and been a world champion—more than once. Born in 1997, Steven Purugganan has accomplished more than most people twice his age—all with just a set of plastic cups.

Sport stacking, in which competitors stack and unstack cups as fast as they can, promotes hand-eye coordination, quickness and focus, self-confidence, teamwork, and good sportsmanship—just as any other sport does. The World Sport Stacking Association, formed as the World Cup Stacking Association in 2001, hosts the World Sport Stacking Championships each spring in Denver, Colorado, verifying world records in age groups and divisions.

In addition to setting records, Purugganan has had a lot of other cool opportunities through sport stacking: as an ambassador of the sport, he has promoted events around the world, been on major television programs, starred in a McDonald's commercial, and been a member of *ESPN Magazine's* Advice Squad.

When not stacking, Purugganan is studying or competing on his high school's cross-country team in New York.

DO YOUR HOMEWORK

Local connections are great, but they will only take you so far. You need to reach out to national organizations too. Check out chapter 11 of this book. It is chock-full of organizations and websites that cover every aspect of working in sports. The internet has made it easier than ever to connect with people around the world, so click that mouse or tap that screen and start exploring! If you have a dream and the determination to work hard to achieve it, the sky is the limit when it comes to your career in sports.

> You can't put a limit on anything. The more you dream, the farther you get.
>
> **Michael Phelps**
> SWIMMER

Note:

1. Tibbals, Geoff. *Ripley's Believe It or Not Sports* (Broomall, PA: Mason Crest Publishers, 2011); Baseball Almanac, Inc., "The Fastest Pitcher in Baseball History," Baseball Almanac, February 2003, http://www.baseball-almanac.com/articles/fastest-pitcher-in-baseball.shtml; and McClintock Brandon. "Aroldis Chapman and the 15 Fastest Pitches Ever Recorded," *Bleacher Report* (April 20, 2011), http://bleacherreport.com/articles/671695-aroldis-chapman-and-the-15-fastest-pitches-ever-recorded.

11

Resources for Sports Careers

ORGANIZATIONS

Academy of Certified Archivists, certifiedarchivists.org

Accrediting Council on Education in Journalism
   and Mass Communications,
   ku.edu/~acejmc/STUDENT/PROGLIST.SHTML

Adventure Cycling Association, adventurecycling.org

Aerobics and Fitness Association of America, afaa.com

Amateur Athletic Union, aausports.org

American Alliance for Health, Physical Education, Recreation
   and Dance, aahperd.org

American Baseball Coaches Association, abca.org

American Board for Certification of Teacher Excellence, abcte.org

American College of Sports Medicine, acsm.org

American Council on Exercise, acefitness.org

American Fitness Professionals and Associates, afpafitness.com

American Institute for Conservation of Historic and Artistic Works, conservation-us.org

American Junior Rodeo Association, ajra.org

American Medical Association, ama-assn.org

American Orthopaedic Society for Sports Medicine, sportsmed.org

American Professional Rodeo Association, aprarodeo.com

American Psychological Association, apa.org

American Red Cross, redcross.org

> Life's this game of inches. So's football. Because in either game, life or football, the margin for error is so small—I mean, one half step too late or too early and you don't quite make it. One half second too slow or too fast, you don't quite catch it. The inches we need are everywhere around us. . . . We fight for that inch. . . . Because we know, when we add up all those inches, that's gonna make the . . . difference between winning and losing, between living and dying.
>
> **Tony D'Amato**
>
> FOOTBALL COACH, *ANY GIVEN SUNDAY*

American School Health
Association, ashaweb.org

American Society of Exercise
Physiologists, asep.org

American Society of Journalists and
Authors, asja.org

American Society of Media
Photographers, asmp.org

American Sportscasters Association,
americansportscastersonline.com

Association for Education in Journalism and Mass
Communication, aejmc.org

Association for Applied Sport Psychology,
appliedsportpsych.org

Athletic Equipment Managers' Association,
equipmentmanagers.org

Barnett Bicycle Institute,
bbinstitute.com

Board of Certification for the Athletic Trainer,
bocatc.org

Broadcast Education Association,
beaweb.org

Center for Sports Administration,
sportsad.ohio.edu

Skiing combines
outdoor fun with
knocking down trees
with your face.

Dave Barry

WRITER

Chronicle of Higher Education, chronicle.com

College and University Professional Association for Human
    Resources, cupahr.org

Cycling Hall of Fame, cyclinghalloffame.com

Fitness.com, fitness.com

Fitness Partner, primusweb.com/fitnesspartner

Harness Racing Museum & Hall of Fame,
    harnessmuseum.com

Harry Wendelstedt Umpire School, umpireschool.com

Hockey Hall of Fame, hhof.com

IDEA Health & Fitness Association, ideafit.com

IMG Worldwide, imgworld.com

International Association of
    Approved Basketball Officials,
    iaabo.org

International Association of Business
    Communicators, iabc.com

International Association of Venue
    Managers, Inc., iavm.org

International Bowling Museum
    & Hall of Fame,
    bowlingmuseum.com

My motto was always to keep swinging. Whether I was in a slump of feeling badly or having trouble off the field, the only thing to do was keep swinging.

Hank Aaron

BASEBALL PLAYER

International Boxing Hall of Fame, ibhof.com

International Facility Management Association, ifma.org

International Gymnastics Hall of Fame, ighof.com

International Swimming Hall of Fame, ishof.org

International Tennis Hall of Fame & Museum,
tennisfame.com

Jim Evans Academy of Professional Umpiring,
umpireacademy.com

Lacrosse Museum & Hall of Fame, uslacrosse.org/topnav/
museumhalloffame/visitthemuseum.aspx

The League of American Bicyclists,
bikeleague.org

Major League Baseball: Umpires, mlb.com/mlb/official_info/
umpires/index.jsp

Major League Baseball Umpire Camps, mlb.com/mlb/
official_info/umpires/camp

Major League Scouting Bureau, mlb.com/careers/index
.jsp?loc=mlbsb

Medical Fitness Association, medicalfitness.org

Naismith Memorial Basketball Hall of Fame,
hoophall.com

National Association for Girls and Women in Sport, aahperd.org/nagws

National Association for Sport and Physical Education, aahperd.org/naspe

National Association of Broadcast Employees & Technicians, nabetcwa.org

National Association of Broadcasters, nab.org

National Association of Collegiate Directors of Athletics, nacda.com

National Association of Collegiate Women Athletics Administrators, nacwaa.org

National Association of Sports Officials, naso.org

National Athletic Trainers' Association, nata.org

National Baseball Hall of Fame and Museum, baseballhall.org

National Basketball Association, nba.com

National Bicycle Dealers Association, nbda.com

National Collegiate Athletic Association, ncaa.org

National Federation of Professional Trainers, nfpt.com

National Football League, nfl.com

National High School Athletic Coaches Association, nhsaca.org

National Museum of Racing and Hall of Fame, racingmuseum.org

National Operating Committee on Standards for Athletic Equipment, nocsae.org

National Press Photographers Association, nppa.org

The National Rowing Foundation's Hall of Fame, natrowing.org/rowing-history/national-rowing-hall-of-fame/

National Soccer Hall of Fame, ussoccer.com/about/history/ hall-of-fame.aspx

National Softball Hall of Fame, asasoftball.com/hall_of_fame/index.asp

National Ski Areas Association, nsaa.org

National Track & Field Hall of Fame, usatf.org/ halloffame

National Wrestling Hall of Fame and Museum, nwhof.org

Newspaper Association of America, naa.org

Newspaper Guild, Communication Workers of America, newsguild.org

Online News Association, onlinenewsassociation.org

PE4life, pe4life.org

PE Central, pecentral.org

Play by Play Sports Broadcasting Camps, playbyplaycamps.com

Professional Photographers of America, ppa.com

Professional Ski Instructors of America, thesnowpros.org

Public Relations Society of America, prsa.org

Pro Football Hall of Fame, profootballhof.com

Radio Television Digital News Association, rtnda.org

Society of American Archivists, archivists.org

Society of Professional Journalists, spj.org

Sports & Fitness Industry Association, sfia.org

Student Photographic Society, studentphoto.com

TeamWork Online LLC, teamworkonline.com

United Bicycle Institute, bikeschool.com

SkiResorts.com, skiresorts.com

SportsCareers, sportscareers.com

> Nobody's a natural. You work hard to get good and then work to get better. It's hard to stay on top.
>
> **Paul Coffey**
>
> HOCKEY PLAYER

SportsShooter, sportsshooter.com

United States Lifesaving Association, usla.org

US Ocean Safety Inc., usos.com

Volleyball Hall of Fame,
  volleyhall.org

Women's Sports Foundation,
  womenssportsfoundation.org

World Figure Skating Museum and Hall of Fame,
  worldskatingmuseum.org

World Golf Hall of Fame,
  worldgolfhalloffame.org

Youth Olympic Games, olympic.org/
  youth-olympic-games

BOOKS AND WEBSITES

The 20 Best Jobs in Sports, bleacherreport.com/
articles/1528393-the-20-best-jobs-in-sports

Aronson, Merry, Don Spetner, and Carol Ames. *The Public Relations Writer's Handbook.* San Francisco: Jossey-Bass, 2007.

Bass, Frank. *The Associated Press Guide to Internet Research and Reporting.* New York: Basic Books, 2002.

Bernhardt, Gale. *Training Plans for Multisport Athletes.* 2nd ed. Boulder, Colorado: VeloPress, 2006.

Brooks, Douglas S. *The Complete Book of Personal Training*. Champaign, Illinois: Human Kinetics, 2003.

Linsenmen, Ciree. *Start Your Own Personal Training Business, 3rd Edition*. Irvine, California: Entrepreneur Press, 2012.

Careers in Sport, topendsports.com/resources/jobs-in-sport.htm

Choosing a Career in Sport, Fitness, and Exercise, americankinesiology.org/careers-in-sport-fitness-and-exercise

Craig, Richard. *Online Journalism: Reporting, Writing, and Editing for New Media*. Belmont, CA: Wadsworth Publishing, 2004.

Dow Jones News Fund: Promoting Careers in Print and Online, newsfund.org

Encyclopedia of Careers and Vocational Guidance. 15th ed. New York: Ferguson Publishing, 2010.

Sedge, Michael. *The Photojournalist's Guide to Making Money*. New York: Allworth Press, 2000.

Foust, James C. *Online Journalism: Principles and Practices of News for the Web*. Scottsdale, Arizona: Holcomb Hathaway Publishers, 2011.

Helitzer, Melvin. *The Dream Job: Sports Publicity, Promotion and Marketing*. 3rd ed. Athens, Ohio: University Sports Press, 1999.

High School Journalism Initiative, hsj.org

Horton, Brian. *The Associated Press Guide to Photojournalism*. 2nd ed. New York: McGraw-Hill, 2000.

John Skilton's baseball-links.com, baseball-links.com

Jones, Charlie. *What Makes Winners Win: Over 100 Athletes, Coaches, and Managers Tell You the Secrets of Success.* New York: Broadway Books, 1998.

Litt, Ann. *Fuel for Young Athletes: Essential Foods and Fluids for Future Champions.* Champaign, IL: Human Kinetics, 2004.

Mack, Gary, with David Casstevens. *Mind Gym: An Athlete's Guide to Inner Excellence.* New York: Contemporary Books, 2001.

O'Brien, Teri S. *The Personal Trainer's Handbook.* 2nd ed. Champaign, IL: Human Kinetics, 2003.

Occupational Outlook Handbook, bls.gov/ooh

Orr, Frank, and George Tracz. *The Dominators: The Remarkable Athletes Who Changed Their Sport Forever.* Toronto: Warwick Publishing Inc., 2004.

Parrish, Fred S. *Photojournalism: An Introduction.* Belmont, CA: Wadsworth Publishing, 2001.

Seitel, Fraser . *The Practice of Public Relations.* 11th ed. Upper Saddle River, NJ: Prentice Hall, 2010.

Starkey, Lauren. *Certified Fitness Instructor/Personal Trainer Career Starter.* New York: LearningExpress, LLC, 2003.

St. Michael, Melyssa, and Linda Formichelli. *Becoming a Personal Trainer for Dummies.* Hoboken, NJ: Wiley Publishing, Inc., 2004.

Thornton, Ed. *It's More Than Just Making Them Sweat: A Career Training Guide for Personal Fitness Trainers.* San Francisco: Robert D. Reed Publishers, 2001.

Yaverbaum, Eric, with Bob Bly. *Public Relations Kit for Dummies.* 2nd ed. Indianapolis, IN: Wiley Publishing, Inc., 2001.

Zavoina, Susan C., and John H. Davidson. *Digital Photojournalism.* Boston: Pearson, 2001.

Zappala, Joseph M., and Ann R. Carden. *Public Relations Worktext: A Writing and Planning Resource.* 3rd ed. New York: Routledge, 2010.

Never put an age limit on your dreams.

Dara Torres

SWIMMER

12

Glossary

amateur. Someone who is not paid for participating in an activity.

bachelor's degree. Degree given by a four-year college or university.

calisthenics. Exercises that promote physical fitness.

cardio. Exercises that raise the heart rate.

certification. Given to people who have completed special training in a field. Tells potential employers that you know what you're doing.

client. Person who is represented by a company.

Division I. Highest level of collegiate sports, followed by Division II and Division III.

draft. To choose a player for a sports organization.

endorsing. Using a product and saying good things about it or allowing a company to use someone's name and image to advertise its products.

extracurricular. Something that is done outside of school, such as belonging to a club or team.

> It's always about wanting to one-up myself from the day before. There's never an absolute 100 percent perfect performance, but going out and striving for that perfect performance is what keeps me going.
>
> **Cat Osterman**
> SOFTBALL PLAYER AND COACH

freelancer. Someone who works for several different companies without being on staff.

independent league. In baseball, professional teams that aren't affiliated with a major league team.

internship. Opportunity to work in an organization and learn what that career is like. Usually arranged through a college or other educational institution. Generally unpaid but can often be used for college credit toward a degree.

MLB. Major League Baseball.

MLS. Major League Soccer.

master's degree. Degree given for study after a bachelor's degree, usually requiring about two years of further study.

median. Number exactly in the middle of a series of numbers.

memorabilia. Items with historical connections, such as equipment used in a major sporting event or owned by a famous athlete.

minor league. In baseball, professional teams where new players can work on their skills or injured or older players can play.

modified sports. Program that makes sports and sports competitions more accessible for younger children and children of different abilities.

NBA. National Basketball Association.

NCAA. National Collegiate Athletic Association, the governing body for all college sports in the United States.

NFL. National Football League.

NHL. National Hockey League.

penalty. Punishment given for breaking the rules.

professional. Someone who is paid for participating in an activity.

rehab. Short for rehabilitation, the process of recovering and regaining strength and skills after an injury or surgery.

referee. Official who makes sure athletes follow the rules during a competition.

scout. Person who looks for new talent to sign to a team.

season. Time of the year when a sport is played.

sponsors. Businesses who pay an athlete's expenses.

sports agent. Someone who represents professional athletes in business and legal opportunities.

sports commentator. Someone who broadcasts a game or sporting event, describing the action.

stamina. Ability to keep doing an activity without getting tired.

statistics. Sets of numbers that provide information about a player or a sport.

stipend. Small payment given to someone for work or to cover expenses.

If the French nobles had been capable of playing cricket with their peasants, their chateaux would never have been burnt.

G. M. Trevelyan
HISTORIAN

A good hockey player plays where the puck is. A great hockey player plays where the puck is going to be.

Wayne Gretzky
HOCKEY PLAYER, COACH, AND EXECUTIVE

umpires. In baseball and hockey, officials who make sure athletes follow the rules during a competition.

WNBA. Women's National Basketball League.

ACKNOWLEDGMENTS

My thanks to everyone who helped me put this book together, especially:

Lindsay Brown and Emmalisa Sparrow from Beyond Words for their awesome list of contacts and their hard work making the many pieces of this book fit together. I couldn't have done any of this without their guidance!

The amazing athletic department at Clarkstown Central School District in New City, New York, especially Tess Brogan, Danielle DeLay, Vince Louther, Tony Mellino, and Edward Benvenuto. Thanks also to Abe Asher, Elizabeth Bennett, Adam Bjaranson, Danielle and Margaret DeStaso, Patsy Jensen; Samantha, Steven, and Sonia Kaner; Garret Kramer, Annelise Loevlie, Joseph Lofberg, Sondra Novak and Howard White from Nike, Ned Rice and the Baltimore Orioles, Kristof Schroeder, Mike Sheridan; Claire, Lydia, and Ann Tembruell; Kevin Tuve and John Burns from the Rockland Boulders baseball team. And to my research assistants and fact checkers: James J., and Leanne and Grace Mattern.

ABOUT THE AUTHOR

Joanne Mattern has never been very good at playing sports, but she has always loved watching them and cheering for her favorite teams. She has been a big baseball fan for most of her life and in later years has learned to love football, hockey, lacrosse, and other sports as well. Joanne is the author of hundreds of books for children, including many sports biographies and books about sports. She lives in New York State with her husband, also an avid sports fan, three daughters who don't like sports at all, and a son who plays lacrosse and whose idea of a great vacation is a trip to the Baseball Hall of Fame.